RETURN FROM
SIBERIA

RETURN FROM
SIBERIA

JOHN SHALLMAN

Skyhorse Publishing

Skyhorse Publishing books may be purchased in bulk at special discounts for sales promotion, corporate gifts, fund-raising, or educational purposes. Special editions can also be created to specifications. For details, contact the Special Sales Department, Skyhorse Publishing, 307 West 36th Street, 11th Floor, New York, NY 10018 or info@skyhorsepublishing.com.

Skyhorse® and Skyhorse Publishing® are registered trademarks of Skyhorse Publishing, Inc.®, a Delaware corporation.

Visit our website at www.skyhorsepublishing.com.

10 9 8 7 6 5 4 3 2 1

Library of Congress Cataloging-in-Publication Data is available on file.

Cover design by Amy Duncan, Target Marketing, and Ray Campbell, Superoxygen

Print ISBN: 978-1-5107-6337-1
Ebook ISBN: 978-1-5107-6340-1

Printed in the United States of America

This book is dedicated to my beloved mother, Saralie Rakow Shallman (1934–2020).

"My grandmother Saralie was pure sweetness—a masterclass in unconditional love, quiet courage, and compassion. You've never met a better listener, or a better judge of character. Grandma was brilliant and beautiful, pragmatic and very funny. Good and kind to her core, thoughtful and full of dignity."

Nina Juliette Barrameda Shallman

Table of Contents

PART II: THE WEST

NOTE TO READER

The story that follows is true, by and large.

It is my family's history.

Certain places, people, and circumstances have been changed or consolidated to streamline the narrative and add drama.

But this mostly happened.

And it changed our lives.

PART I

THE EAST

Chapter 1

Ancestors

She threw the line out like a fisherman: "Each one of us came from some-where else." Quickly, but with stealth. Testing the waters. Hoping for a bite. None was forthcoming.

John Simon bit his lip, worried this might happen. He surveyed the crowd like a litigator reading a jury. Was anyone on their side?

"It's what all of us have in common," the woman continued, holding the podium with both hands as if trying to steer it in the right direction. "We're all strangers to this land."

Migrants! John winced. *Migrants to this land* was the line he wrote. Rookie politicians never stick to the script. Number one job hazard. This particular transgression was not that big a deal. But sometimes a client goes rogue on a single word and suddenly it becomes a demeaning meme on social media. Then everyone blames the communications guy.

John prided himself on being very good at his job—a policy wonk, with an encyclopedic knowledge of all things political. But he had trou-ble sometimes being taken seriously—due to the fact that, despite his forty-plus years, John could still pass for a teenager were it not for his red Van Dyke beard. Accepting with chagrin that he'd likely be carded at liquor stores for life, John knew many folks would die to have his genes, which made him grudgingly thankful. He also felt gratitude about being able to make a living doing something he loved—politics, particularly in the throes of a long-odds race like this one. In moments like these, John felt like a defensive coordinator for the underdog team at the Super Bowl. It was all about staying focused and calling the right plays.

John scanned his phone to see if people were live-tweeting the speech—unlikely, given the underwhelming crowd. But one never knew. There were sixty-five in attendance—few enough to count by hand. Not that he had. He knew the number within seconds of their arrival. In his two decades as a political consultant, John had developed the ability to guess the size of a crowd with uncanny accuracy. He could also read their political leanings, predict laughs, applause lines, and standing ovations. That wasn't going to happen anytime soon. People were standing. But clapping? No.

"Our parents came from somewhere else," said the Latina at the microphone. "Or our grandparents, or our great-grandparents." She paused, noticing a cluster of Native Americans eyeing her with reserve from one corner of the grassy field. John had spotted them, too. Karankawa, he suspected, or Comanche. Clearly outliers in this predominantly Hispanic crowd, along with the five bikers and two dozen rednecks, curious but unlikely to be swayed. John swiveled back to the stage, wondering why his client had stopped speaking. She's flustered by the Comanche, he guessed. *Don't do it*, he pleaded mentally—*stick to the script.*

She couldn't help herself. "Even indigenous people moved from time to time, when food was scarce. And this beautiful land—Mother Earth welcomed them."

Mother Earth? John frowned. *Don't go New Age. You'll lose everybody.*

"That's what happened to me in my time of need. This great country opened her arms and took me in, which is why I can proudly say to you today that my name is Patricia Alvarado and I am running for Congress."

Polite applause. It was better than boos. You gotta start somewhere.

The crowd dispersed, and a cute schoolgirl—in plaited hair and a pleated skirt—approached the platform. "Can I get a picture with you, Ms. Alvarado?"

"Call me Patti," said the candidate, flashing her contagious smile.

"Stand by the statue," John intervened, positioning them near the memorial for the singer Selena, a local landmark he'd carefully curated for its symbolic resonance. Selena, the Queen of Tejano music, was adored by the Hispanic community for having busted through barriers in the male-dominated Tex-Mex music scene. Patti had brought white roses, Selena's favorite, to the monument overlooking Corpus Christi Bay. And now she retrieved one of those flowers as a gift to her school-girl fan before taking the selfie. The girl beamed. Patti worked her pearly whites, framed by that perfect shade of lipstick.

Camera sure loves her, thought John. Patti had passion in spades, along with undeniable charisma. She was attractive and young, just shy of forty. Magnetic, a go-getter. Everything you needed in a candidate. While her experience in politics was slim—hence her reliance on John—having a blank slate was often better than having a bad record. And no one's record was nearly as atrocious as that of her opponent, Ralph Trent, the eight-term incumbent in Texas' 27th District.

Trent was, without exaggeration, to the right of Attila the Hun. John found his politics repugnant. Trent had called for LGBTQ intern-ment camps, so that "those folks could do their business out of public view." Yep—Ralph Trent proudly went on the record with that one. His A+ rating from the NRA sat in a spit-shined frame on Trent's mahogany desk, alongside hero shots of Barry Goldwater, David Duke, and George Lincoln Rockwell, founder of the American Nazi Party. Ralph Trent was rabidly anti-immigrant. He once made incendiary remarks calling for federally sanctioned lynchings of illegal aliens along the border as a way to dissuade new asylum seekers, just as Ancient Romans used to line their city walls with Jews on crucifixes.

Provocation was Trent's *modus operandi*—the more extreme, the more the media attacked him, and the more his base rallied around him. That was the Ralph Trent playbook. He'd been at it long before the Trump era. And it worked. Trent had been a shoe-in in his district for almost two decades—in fact, his colleagues in Congress called it the "Ralph Trent Seat."

When John Simon happened upon a local news story in early 2018 about an unknown Latina announcing her intention to unseat Ralph Trent, he caught the next plane to Texas. It was his kind of fight: the classic underdog. Her picture grabbed him right away: a determined gaze that jumped off the page. There was wisdom in that face. Nothing forced, just a natural appeal.

When John met Patti, along with her husband, Enrique, at the Corpus Christi airport, they had him at *Hola*. They were warm, friendly, and impossible not to like. Enrique was comfortable with allowing his wife to shine and greeted John like an old friend. Patti brought homemade tamales their daughter prepared from an old family recipe. Enrique grabbed John's bag, so he could have a bite of tamale on the way to the car. People were starting to recognize Patti from her picture in the paper, coming up to shake her hand. Men were slapping Enrique on the back. And John had an epiphany.

This might just work.

Then again, woe to the man who thinks he knows the electorate. How many times in recent years had John had that feeling—*this might just work*—and faced humiliation on Election Day? There was the Senate race in Nevada, where John was polishing their victory speech after the local news had called it, only to have the Republican-heavy absentee ballots come in late and pull the rug out from under them. And that affordable housing measure in California where developers had outspent them by a hundred to one and they still came within striking distance—a real heartbreak, though most of his colleagues thought he should have seen it coming.

John had developed a reputation as the Don Quixote of political consultants—or worse, the Broadway Danny Rose, putting on a brave face and working behind the scenes for laughing-stock candidates who didn't have a prayer. And yet, he couldn't help himself.

John had a soft spot for taking on the most daunting challenges, the longest of longshots—and this 2018 House race for Texas's 27th Congressional Seat was exactly that. A long shot. The district—which had been redrawn and gerrymandered so drastically that it looked (befitting, for Texas) like a T-bone steak—stretching along the Gulf Coast from Corpus Christi to Lake Jackson, and then inland to San Marcos. While squarely Republican, it had a significant Latino population, which had been largely marginalized as a voting bloc. That's where John saw the opportunity for Patti Alvarado—pitting a fiery female from Mexico against a right-wing white male who was zealously anti-immigrant. But it's not just that Patti was Mexican, it's that she had crossed the border illegally fourteen years prior and only established her US citizenship recently by marrying Enrique, a naturalized Mexican-American. This was unprecedented—a former undocumented immigrant running for Congress, which is what made the proposition so enticing for John: the ultimate David and Goliath fight, one that the press should find irresistible. But talk about a Hail Mary.

John's wife, Lani, mother of his four children and a pragmatist if there ever was one, had been hesitant about the idea. Another high-profile loss could potentially jeopardize his reputation—and Lani was fiercely protective of all her loved ones' reputations, especially her husband's. But a win—as far-fetched as it seemed—could cement the reputation that John had had at the start of his career—as a political visionary. And that was ultimately enough to convince her.

After the speech in front of the Mirador de la Flor memorial for Selena, Patti and Enrique invited John back to their home, where they were having a special family gathering before the *quinceañera* of Patti's daughter, Alexa, scheduled for the following day. John was touched and honored to be included—it was also deeply illuminating.

While Alexa was Patti's daughter from a previous marriage, she had been completely embraced by four generations of Enrique's family. There were at least forty relatives in attendance, filling every nook and cranny of the ranch home, which Enrique, who worked in construction, had proudly built himself. He took John around from room to room, introducing him to cousins, aunts, and grandparents, while pointing out details of the craftsmanship, such as the traditional earthen floor—a mixture of clay, sand, and fiber, compacted and cured with linseed oil, which, along with the adobe walls, kept the house relatively cool in the summer. While John was impressed by the house, it was the atmosphere that really warmed his heart.

There was music and laughter in every room. Multicolored light strands soared over the yard, where the food was plentiful and increasing by the minute. In the kitchen, Alexa and her three aunts were making their traditional tamales in a joyous production line, while Uncle Jaime played a Mexican accordion to one side. Patti handed John a margarita and took him by the hand to meet the family matriarch—Enrique's *abuelita* Maria, still going strong in her nineties, with an infectious, toothless grin.

"Isn't she precious?" Patti whispered in John's ear. "Take a selfie," said John. "For Twitter."

"Don't have my phone," she deflected. "Use mine," he insisted.

"No phones. It's family time."

"You sound like my wife," John smirked. "Your wife sounds wise." He nodded.

"Are your grandparents still with us?" Patti asked him. John shook his head. All but one died before he was born.

"Too bad," she gazed at him with empathy. "Where we come from is important. It's our history."

A slight melancholy came over John, as he gazed across the yard at the vibrant Alvarado clan. Patti asked if he could stay one more day—to be part of Alexa's *quinceañera*. John told her he had to get back to Los Angeles. Patti nodded—family comes first.

Family had everything to do with John's career in politics. John grew up in a liberal, secular Jewish home, the second youngest of five, in Rock Island, Illinois—population: 38,000, about 150 miles west of Chicago. His grandmother, Rose, who'd emigrated from Russia, was also part of the household. And the women in his life had a major influence on his world-view. His mother, having named him after JFK, instilled the values of service and giving back—particularly to one's community. So it was only natural for John to aspire to public service. It began his junior year of high school, when John was elected to serve as the student member of the school board of Rock Island-Milan School District #41. He was sixteen, barely out of braces when he showed up in a suit and tie for his first board meeting. With his keen intellect and good ideas, John held his own in the school board meetings, where the adult members, the youngest of which had two decades on him, must have wondered—has he even started shaving? The answer was: yes. In fact, over the summer John could grow sufficient hair on his face to vaguely resemble a beard and age him just enough to purchase beer from Lenny, a stoner at Lee's liquor store, who gave him "a pass for growing a 'stache." This way, he didn't have to keep pulling out of his Velcro wallet his older brother's expired driver's license every time his friends wanted a six-pack. But Mr. Allison, his football coach and a former Marine, made sure his players were clean-shaven, with crew cuts before the first day of practice. And so that dreadful day at the barbershop on 18th Avenue came, sending John back in time, revealing his prepubescent baby face that was on full display at the board meeting. He looked more like a nervous Bar Mitz-vah boy than a member of the board of education.

John always arrived fifteen minutes early for the school board meet-ings with a clean shirt and a fresh pad of paper, values drilled into him by his father, who worked for the Department of Defense. "Always show up like you mean business," his dad would say. "And if you're on time, you're late."

The other board members warmed up to John eventually. But then came … the showdown. The debate over the 1990 budget, which had just been slashed by the legislature, leaving them little choice: either increase class sizes dramatically; cut sports, music, and arts programs; or lay-off 20 percent of the district's teachers. As the council began the difficult debate, John asked to be recognized by the chairman, a retiree in his seventies, who nodded. Seven adults turned to watch sixteen-year-old John Simon give his first political address.

"If we're about to choose between firing teachers or cramming more desks into already crowded classrooms, here's how I'm going to vote: Neither."

"We don't have the funds…," began the chairman with an air of disdain.

"Yeah, funding's always the issue, isn't it?" John continued. "So it's pretty simple then. All we need to do is find some more money."

The condescending expressions were spreading, but they didn't faze him. John had done his homework. He had a simple proposal: increase local property taxes by one quarter of one percent, and they'd have more than enough money to fund the school district budget. He'd drawn up language for a referendum that they could add as a local ballot initiative in November.

The chairman snickered. John made an impassioned plea, "We must do this on behalf of the children. YOU have had your chance, but WE only get one chance at a good education." He milked that last line, a skill he perfected while appearing in a few high school drama productions as a sophomore. Mrs. Rowland, his drama teacher, would have been proud. John managed to coax other board members to go along with his plan. It passed four to three. Now he just needed to persuade the electorate.

He had two things in his favor: 1) he was a student in the district, and 2) he had a bike. John figured he'd use the same playbook that got him elected to the school board: going door to door.

After canvassing for a day with a heavy stack of fliers in the U-Haul box that he'd jerry-rigged to his tail rack, John had already clocked twenty-six miles—the length of a marathon. That's when he had deep regrets about rolling through that stop sign on his recent driving test. But the kid on his hand-me-down, ten-speed Raleigh bicycle riding neighborhood to neighborhood like Paul Revere to save the schools was picked up by several local news outlets, including WQAD News 8, which decided to send up their traffic chopper for an aerial shot. From Lincoln to Longview Park, from Harris Pizza to Whitey's Ice Cream, pretty soon people were applauding him as he rode by with a caravan of fellow students joining the cause, handing out flyers and waving signs. And, to everyone's amazement, the referendum passed.

When John took his place that night at the dinner table, his four siblings got up and gave him a standing ovation. His mother was in tears, and his dad came around to pat him proudly on the back. But the moment that deeply impacted John—where he had an epiphany of a life dedicated to public service—was at school the following day, when Mrs. Emerson, his ninth-grade history teacher, walked up to John, welling with emotion, and thanked him.

"You saved my job," she said. "My mother was a teacher here, and her mother before her. I don't know what I would have done if I couldn't teach at Rocky. You saved my career, John Simon." She cried and hugged him with all of her heart. And John would never be the same.

He had seen firsthand how good public policy and a good political campaign could have a profound impact on people's lives. And how anyone, no matter who or how young they were, could make a difference. It wasn't just the students who had benefited from his campaign, it was the entire community. The meaning of his life was coming into focus—past, present, future were all in alignment, the trajectory consistent and clear. Being named after John F. Kennedy … becoming president of the Student Senate his senior year … founding the debate club at school … getting an A+ in Honors US History, running for the board of education, passing the referendum. It was suddenly obvious.

He was on his way to becoming president of the United States.

That didn't quite pan out for John. His boyhood fantasy notwithstanding,

John quickly realized he was just as effective working behind the scenes on message and strategy. Building on his high school reputation, John worked on political races as an intern and later as a speechwriter throughout his time as a student at the University of Iowa, where his father earned his PhD and where John spent summers at former Olympic gold medalist Dan Gable's wrestling camps. Iowa City was a beautiful college town just fifty-five miles east on I-80 from Rock Island. John's years at Iowa were formative, and his writing skills were honed in a place where presidential politics and great writing merged. His cousin, David—a legend in Iowa City Democratic political circles—recruited John to work on a long-shot presidential campaign for a US senator from California, which eventually led him to his first real job in Los Angeles and a series of winning campaigns that paved the way for a successful young career as a political consultant.

After his flight landed in Burbank, John retrieved his blue-gray '66 Ford Mustang from valet parking. This was his father's car that he restored after it sat for years in his parent's garage in Rock Island. The windshield still displayed a dozen vehicle tax decals dating back to the 1976 Bicentennial celebration, with images of the Centennial Bridge that connected Iowa and Illinois across the mighty Mississippi River. Like tattoos, John didn't have the heart to remove any, as they served as daily reminders of his Midwestern small-town values while traversing the freeways and boulevards of Tinsel Town.

He drove home to Encino just in time for "MFD" (mandatory family dinner)—a monthly ritual that John's wife, Lani, had instituted several years back, requiring all four kids (including the two girls, who'd flown the coop) to return home on the first Saturday of every month. Rose, the eldest at twenty-three (named after the one grandparent that John had known), went to grad school locally, so that was easy enough. Juliette, twenty-one, was at Amherst but happened to be home for winter break (when at school, she still had to FaceTime in for the occasion). MFD was sacred.

Lani, who worked part-time in advertising in addition to running the household, volunteering at school, and raising four kids, allowed "Hall Passes" from time to time for the girls—understanding that college life had its own set of demands. But Rose and Juliette showed up by and large—appreciating their mother's efforts to keep them connected to the boys, Joseph and Samuel, who were considerably younger.

The four kids and two dogs converged like a rugby team as their father walked in that evening with his roll-on bag. John gave them each a set of maracas he had bought in the Corpus Christi *Mercado*, and the house was soon enveloped in a joyous cacophony just like the Alvarados. John met Lani's gaze. She was his bedrock—a consistent and unflagging source of support. Despite dramatic differences in their backgrounds, they seemed to interlock like odd pieces of a jigsaw puzzle. John was Jewish, raised in Rock Island, Illinois; Catholic Lani grew up in Vallejo, California, with parents who were from the Philippines. Yet both came from large families, where they were second-to-last in birth order—the reason, perhaps, for their unexpected compatibility.

Dinner was brisket, a family favorite (Lani had used the secret John had learned from his mother, Saralie—adding instant onion soup mix to tenderize the meat). There was much to discuss. John reported on his trip to Texas. Lani briefed John on her talk with Rabbi Weiss in which they settled on November 3 as the day for Joseph's bar mitzvah. John blanched slightly. *Wouldn't you know it—three days before Election Day! Of course, Rabbi Weiss always made a point to schedule the bar or bat mitzvahs as close to the child's thirteenth birthday as possible. It just so happened that Joseph's birthday was that week.*

Lani caught his expression—she never missed a beat.

John, deflecting, jumped in with a question for Joseph: "Have you been given your *Parsha*?"

"*Toldot*," responded the twelve-year-old, who had dark eyes like his mother. Then he added, both nervous and proud: "Part of Genesis."

"What's a *Parsha*—isn't that a sports car?" asked Samuel, the youngest at age ten—impish, adorable, and a wisecracker. John explained that, at his bar mitzvah, Joseph would be leaving his boyhood behind to become an active member of the synagogue. He'll lead the service—not only reading that week's portion of the Torah in Hebrew, but also offering his interpretation of its meaning.

"But he doesn't speak Hebrew," said Samuel, stating the obvious.

Lani smiled. "That's why he goes to Hebrew school. Now Joseph has nine months to learn his *Parsha*." Despite her Catholic upbringing, she'd consented to John's desire to raise their kids as Jews. However, since Judaism is matrilineal, children trace their Jewish descent through their mothers—so each one of the Simon kids had to convert.

Jewish tradition prescribes a profound symbol for this process. The candidate must place him- or herself in a radically different physical environment—in water rather than air, fully submerged and naked, not touching any of the walls or the floor of the *mikveh* bathing font. This leaves the person floating, momentarily suspended without breathing—as if in the womb, which primes you symbolically for a rebirth. The boys jumped in with gusto, embracing the curious ritual, as did Juliette, albeit with a bit of trepidation. But Rose balked—too weird for her.

"I'm Jewish," she declared. And that was the end of it.

As tradition would have it, MFD was capped the following morning with a Sunday visit to Grandma Saralie's house, about fifteen minutes away from the Simons in Woodland Hills. After a lifetime in Chicago and later in Rock Island, John's parents, Bill and Saralie, relocated to Southern California, where he lived, along with his sister and two brothers. Saralie, spritely and full of energy, despite her eight decades on the planet, greeted the Simon clan with enthusiasm. She had prepared the usual spread—fresh bagels from Brent's Deli, along with lox, smoked whitefish, sliced tomatoes, red onions, capers, and three flavors of cream cheese. The boys attacked the spread like wild animals; the adults waded over to the coffee thermos. Saralie asked John about the race in Texas, smiling at him as if he were still the sixteen-year-old boy saving schools in Illinois.

"We still have a long way to go, Mom," said John, exchanging a glance with Lani.

"It'll work out exactly the way it's meant to," replied his mother with the wisdom befitting a life lived with grace.

Joseph blurted through his bagel-filled mouth: "My skate party!"

"Oh, yes," remembered Lani. "Joe's been invited to an ice-skating birthday at Iceland in Van Nuys. I thought it would be cool for him to try out his dad's old skates if you still have them around."

Saralie lit up. "Let's take a look after we eat."

After he scarfed down two and a half bagels with shmeer, Joseph joined his parents and Saralie in her sprawling attic, which was filled with items of every description—books, trinkets, memorabilia. John looked around, shaking his head in amusement at the clutter that was screaming: garage sale! But Saralie was not planning to part with her trove anytime soon. Back in Rock Island, her ephemeral collection had filled the entire basement; Saralie forced the movers, to John's chagrin, to box every last item for shipment to California, where, by virtue of the fact that no one has basements in LA, it had ended up above the house.

With its cobwebs, creaking floorboards, and dust particles in the shafts of sunlight streaming through gabled windows—Saralie's attic could have been a movie set. Little Joseph ran his fingers along the dusty shelves, perusing the relics in fascination, while John experienced a wave of nostalgia, seeing his old debate trophies, football and wrestling medals, and other long-forgotten reminders of his youth. Lani, with her eagle eyes, spotted the skates, half-buried in a box of old shoes. "Size nine," she said. "Perfect."

She turned to Joseph. But the adolescent hadn't registered what she said.

Her son was mesmerized by an item in front of him—a book. Nearly one hundred years old:

Exiled in Siberia by Joseph Rakow.

"Who's Joseph Rakow?" asked the twelve-year-old.

"Your great-grandfather," said John, moving over in sudden interest.

"It's who you were named after." He turned to his mother: "I never knew he wrote a book?"

"Ah, yes," Saralie took a breath, and nodded. "His memoir— self-published … after moving to Chicago and marrying Grandma Rose."

The three adults converged around Joseph as he opened the cover and peered inside to see a photograph of his unknown ancestor opposite the title page—a handsome man, rugged, pensive, with dark eyes and a tender heart. Little Joseph could only imagine what stories would unfold within the chapters of his great-grandfather's book. But, in turning the pages, he was met with something unexpected.

The entire manuscript was in Yiddish.

CHAPTER 2

COMRADE RAKŌW

What follows is a journal of my life—the moments and circumstances that shaped me into becoming a lifelong revalutsyaner (revolutionary) in the struggle of workers against oppression by the ruling class. In my Russian homeland, I experienced betrayal, heartbreak, and grave injustice—conditions that led, eventually, to the Russian Revolution. I was surprised, however, at how many of the same conditions carried over to my adopted land of America. These themes, I've come to realize, are universal.

In that way, I hope that my journey may serve as a roadmap for others.

I was born in the small Jewish-Russian Ukrainian shtetl (townlet) of Telekhan in the year 1888. My father, Avrom, was from an orthodox family and, until the last year of his life, was involved in the construction of houses and bridges. At the age of six, my father wrapped me in a talis (prayer shawl) and carried me to the kheyder (elementary religious school) of the rebe (teacher) Yoyne.

Yoyne the melamed sat quite at ease at the long wooden table, surrounded by a dozen boys, and quite calmly kept fingering his long, broad, black beard. Upon seeing me he offered a hearty sholem aleykhem (greeting: peace be with you), sat me down at the table, and, without the slightest delay, began to teach me from his curriculum.

His method began, naturally, with teaching the alphabet. "Alef," he intoned. I repeated after him: "beyz." "Giml" (ABC). And here something amazed me—as soon as I repeated his "giml," I heard a clink and a shining penny landed from on high, settling on my prayer book as though it had fallen from the ceiling.

The children, the other students of rebe Yoyne, grew rapturous over the penny and began clapping their hands, and the rebe himself, seeing how amazed and astounded I had become, began to explain to me that it was an angel of G-d that had dropped the gift to me so that I would be a good boy and study with great desire and zeal. And if I would be good and pious, the angel would probably often toss me more gifts...

Truth be told, I remained somewhat skeptical about the rebe's explanation because, when the second penny fell, I noticed that, somehow, my father's hand was over my head ... but I did not dwell on the matter, as my naïveté, mixed with fear, was directed at the rebe, at his stern gaze and his hairy face.

I didn't learn much in the first term at my kheyder. Still, when the term ended, I was able to read a bit of ivre (Biblical Hebrew). I was also not much of a scholar, and, generally, the kheyder wasn't much more than a hardship, and I was delighted when evening came and I could go out to play. And, as my father was a builder, I also loved to play at building; I would try to build wood chips and shavings into "houses" and other structures of my imagination.

My older brother, Max, helped me also in that regard, when he taught me to whittle larger pieces of wood with a penknife. Max was two years older and I looked up to him with awe. He always had great plans and ambitions. And he would describe his dreams late at night in the bunk that we shared, when everyone else was asleep—of travels to exotic lands and magnificent accomplishments.

"In America there are buildings so tall they scrape the sky," Max whispered. I was mesmerized.

Max showed me, one day, how to carve a little log into the form of a rook from the chess set. It took great patience and skill to make it perfectly round, with a wider base and circular parapets up top with crenels chipped out for our imaginary archers. After laboring for hours, passing the penknife back and forth—for we only had one to share between us—we would set our miniature towers on the corner of the table. Then Max and I would lie on the ground looking up at the table from below, so our little creations appeared to soar upward like real towers at the corners of mighty palaces.

In moments like this, I felt invincible.

There was another leaning I had in those years—at the very beginning of my childhood I had an inclination toward music. I had no fiddle; I couldn't begin to dream of the means of obtaining a real fiddle, as my fantasies could not reach to such heights. So I obtained bits of twine, drew them across a makeshift wooden soundboard, and tried to coax notes from them that were, of course, closer to screeching than to music.

The sounds of this fiddle with its twine strings did not satisfy me, and I began to seek means of improving my instrument so that it might produce better notes. Max gave me the idea that hairs from a horse's tail would far better serve my purpose. And the chase after horses' tails began. I wasn't alone in this chase, but an entire company of my fellow kheyder boys set out across the shtetl in search of a musical horse.

When we did manage to engage with such a guest, the horse suffered mightily at our hands. We would steal up on him from behind and grab handfuls of his tail. The beast would pitifully kick its rear hooves and leap in all directions, but we would pay it no mind.

We might have torn out all its tail were it not for the intervention of my mother, Sophie, who gently pulled me aside and instilled some compassion in my self-involved, preadolescent mind—which did not fathom the fact that the poor horse was a sentient being, too.

My mother was the kindest person I have ever known, always helping those in need. This generous nature of hers was a stabilizing force in our family, for it gave us the sense that, even in times of great scarcity (of which there were many), if we were kind to others, the world would always provide us with exactly what we needed. No more, no less. Just enough.

Yanking the hair from the tail of an innocent horse was certainly not an act of kindness. But, I must confess, I secretly held on to those hairs I had harvested. The suggestion from Max had piqued my curiosity as to whether the horsehairs would produce a better note on my makeshift fiddle. While it is true that I obtained nicer notes than from the twine, they in no way sounded like the notes of a real violin, and I did not derive much joy from the horsetail strings. To have my own violin was not meant to be. Who could possibly have dreamt of such an extraordinary luxury?

When I was about eight years old, we left the shtetl of Telekhan and settled in Pinsk. Our entire family then consisted of two boys, one girl, and our parents. My eldest sibling and only sister, Sonya, was twelve years old. I was the third child born to my parents.

In Pinsk we lived in a wooden house that my father had built himself with his own proletarian hands. However, I spent little time in the house, because my father placed me at once into the town's talmud toyre (Talmud Torah, secondary religious school), where I studied from early morning until late at night.

A talmud toyre in a shtetl was not like what we in America might imagine it to be. The teachers at the talmud toyre were coarse fellows, devoid of knowledge, without the slightest idea how to teach children or inspire them. They beat us mercilessly and instead of encouraging the love of learning, they fostered a climate of fear, and, as a result, we developed hatred toward the teachers and the curriculum.

I am reminded of an incident:

Once I needed to leave the classroom to get a drink of water. I forgot to ask the teacher for permission. Upon my return the rabbi approached me and without any warning began to beat me with his cane so unmercifully that I doubled over and shrieked. The rabbi was unconcerned; in fact, he enjoyed it. The more I sobbed, the clearer became his sadism and the harder he beat me.

This was in the first term of my attendance at the talmud toyre. It left a terrible impression on me. Even more hurtful than the pain was the feeling that I had been dealt with unjustly, which for me was the deepest of transgressions. When I returned home that night I had made a decision about the talmud toyre. The following morning, when I was to go to school, I told my mother that I would no longer go there. It was the first time in my life that I had taken a stance for my own rights. My mother's persuasions were of no avail; of no use, either, were my father's threats. I felt triumphant: my childish soul had revolted against an injustice—I won my first strike!

My parents still desired me to have at least some familiarity with the "little letters," that I might at least be able to write a letter in Yiddish. So they hired a Hebrew-Yiddish teacher for me, a "writer," as he was called, who began coming to our house to teach me and my older brother, Max.

But, though I had a natural ability at acquiring vocabulary, I soon lost interest in the "writer." I was about eleven years old then and didn't want to learn anything. My father tried to convince me with both arguments and punishment, but to no avail. I wanted to become a "master" of a trade, not a master of letters—a builder like my father was, and like Max was learning to be.

Perhaps, had my father been more insistent with me, forcing me to study, my stubbornness might have broken. But the needs of our household were so great that he could not really afford tuition. Poverty in our house was quite deep—our income was very small. In addition, my father was in debt that he had assumed in building our house. I knew how to drive nails and also knew how to hold a hammer—so in a short time I became my father's helper, joining Max, who was already his apprentice.

When I reached the age of thirteen my father led me, on my birthday, to the synagogue. My zeyde (grandfather), Naftoli, was the temple shamash (the "Sexton," who helped to run the service). I was called up to read the Torah, and for the first time in my life, I was draped in a talis (prayer shawl). After I pronounced the blessings, my zeyde placed his hands on me and blessed me. For a short time after becoming barmitsve (bar mitzvah, son of the commandment), I attended the synagogue every day. But that did not last long. I became interested in something entirely different—you could say almost the opposite of our ancient Judaic religion: the Russian Revolutionary Movement.

I'd become acquainted with this percolating underground rebellion through my sister, Sonya, who was eighteen at the time and working grueling hours at a factory that manufactured matches. She'd leave the house before dawn and not return until after midnight, coughing and sometimes crying herself to sleep, with blistered hands and broken spirits. She'd been introduced to revolutionary ideas by her friend Minne, who also worked in that nightmarish factory, where laborers had been secretly circulating a banned book, *The Communist Manifesto*, which advocated for the rights of workers. An underground revolutionary storm had begun to grip the Jewish working class. Clandestine "Bundist" labor organizations were springing up throughout Russia.

The Bund, which was both a labor federation and an underground political party, exerted extraordinary moral influence on the Jewish working class and on Jewish intellectuals. Its influence was especially pronounced in our city, Pinsk, where the Bund conducted propaganda among the workers, calling them to struggle for a just social order and a better future. The Bund had also pulled off an extraordinary feat: eliminating the well-known protsar provocateur Aaron Notski—a daring terrorist act, which put them under the glare of the elite and ruthless Cossack guards, who patrolled the streets on horseback with their deadly sabers.

Following the assassination of Notski, who'd been responsible for the torture and death of dozens of labor leaders, the Bund pulled off a second heroic act that resonated across the city: the freeing from jail of the Bundist activist Tepper, his wife, and several other revolutionaries. All of this made a tremendous impression on my idealistic young mind. I wanted to get closer to these noble revolutionaries, who roamed the streets at night, shoving printed proclamations under window shutters, calling on the "Workers Everywhere to Unite!" The enticing pamphlets were signed by "The Jewish Workers' Bund of Lithuania, Poland, and Russia."

I wanted to become better acquainted with these heroic fighters, to look at them, and understand their cause. I felt camaraderie with my sister and the other revolutionaries based on my own experience of having rebelled against the sadistic rabbis at my talmud toyre, but Sonya was completely secretive about her activities.

She would often disappear all evening long, and she would never tell us where she was going or where she had been. Her attitude was strange and incomprehensible to me. The more that Sonya hid her secrets from me and from our entire household, the more I became interested in discovering where she was going—even though I was aware of how dangerous it must have been.

Once—when everyone was fast asleep—I noticed Sonya and Minne, who had spent the night with us, dress quietly and leave the house. As soon as they left I awoke Max, and the two of us began to follow them.

We had to be very secretive in our surveillance, for the girls stopped at every corner, checking in each direction to make sure they were not being followed. We stealthily jumped over several fences, as they did, and finally arrived at an old barn at the edge of town. Sonya and Minne snuck up to an entrance on one side, where they rapped on the door using a special code— knock ... pause ... three quick taps.

My heart was beating like a drum as we watched from the shadows. A tall revolutionary, whose bearded face was covered in a red bandana, opened the door and admitted Sonya and Minne, who saluted him with raised fists. He had a revolver and checked outside before bolting the door shut.

Max and I exchanged nervous glances. We'd come this far—we simply had to see what was inside that barn. My courageous brother led the way, and we slithered up to the door. Max took a deep breath and tried the secret code.

After a moment, the door creaked open, and we were scrutinized by the armed guard who peered suspiciously at us over his bandana.

"How old are you?" he demanded.

"I'm eighteen," lied Max without hesitation. "My brother is sixteen." He had smoothly added three years to our ages, then boldly improvised: "We know how to build bombs." My pulse raced in shock at what my brother had just said, but I tried to remain calm, as the guard looked me in the eyes. After what seemed like an eternity, he finally nodded and waved us through.

I cannot begin to describe my elation as we entered the barn, where hundreds of revolutionaries were gathered in solidarity. There was a large banner across the stage, printed in Yiddish and Russian: Long live the eight-hour workday! Down with the capitalist system! Long live Socialism! We spotted Sonya near the front, standing alongside the movement's leaders, and our hearts were filled with pride for her, along with a sense of joy and hope for our collective future.

Everyone in the room was on their feet, standing tall with clenched fists over their hearts, singing with fervor the opening words of the rousing anthem to workers everywhere—known as "The Internationale":

> Stand up, all victims of oppression,
> To the tyrants who fear your might!
> Don't cling so hard to your possessions,
> For you have nothing if you have no rights!
> Let racist ignorance be ended,
> For respect makes the empires fall!
> Freedom is merely privilege extended,
> Unless enjoyed by one and all.

Max and I looked at each other, our eyes clouded by tears of rapture and pride, as the chanting continued, getting louder and more passionate with every stanza. We made a youthful pact that night—we would be revolutionaries for life, not stopping the fight until all workers everywhere were free.

Chapter 3

Decoding the Past

John's eldest daughter, Rose, had devoured the first translated chapter of *Exiled in Siberia*, along with everyone else in the household, intrigued by this great-grandfather they had never met. All she knew was that the family had emigrated from Russia one hundred years prior—presumably to find a better life. Now she had a graphic sense of the dire conditions they'd left behind. It was strangely comforting. It made her feel more grounded, somehow.

"We learn from our ancestors," said her boyfriend, Bijan, an Iranian national who was studying philosophy at UCLA, where his father was a visiting scholar of Sufi poetry.

"Those are the stories we told one another for millennia around our campfires—the adventures of those who came before. So we could try to make sense of this crazy thing called 'the human condition.'" Bijan gazed out at the Pacific, and Rose put her arm around him, wondering—*Where did you come from?* He smiled at her. Rose, like her sister, Juliette, had inherited the thick, black hair and Eurasian eyes of their mother.

Her connection to Bijan had been instant. Nine months ago, when they had met at the outdoor Cinco de Mayo festivities on Olvera Street, they'd gone deep within minutes—a hypnotic discussion of the Jungian Archetypes that all cultures seem to share.

Bijan had shown up at the *Mercado* with his soccer buddies, Rose with two girlfriends she'd known since middle school. But they both quickly abandoned the respective posses of wingpeople to continue their mesmerizing tête-à-tête. Bijan explained his fascination that, whether we come from Persia or Paris, whether we're Muslims or Jews, young or old—when we dream, we seem to enter a realm that Jung claimed was common to and shared by all of us.

Rose was right there with him. As a painter exploring a postmodern style that included touches of surrealism, she drew significant inspiration from her dreams. Ever since she'd taken a high school elective on "Carl Jung & Joseph Campbell"—a class that officially rocked her world—her dream journal was always ready at her bedside. Bijan, proud owner of a highly dog-eared and annotated copy of *A Hero with a Thousand Faces*, was likewise enthralled with Campbell.

Then—Bijan quoted Rumi (one of Rose's favorites):

Out beyond ideas of wrongdoing and rightdoing there is a field.
I'll meet you there.

Where did you come from?, she thought—looking into Bijan's dark and thoughtful eyes.

Both of them loved the ocean, so that summer was marked by frequent excursions up Pacific Coast Highway for weekend picnics at Paradise Cove. They continued the tradition through the fall and winter—the coastal "Driveaway," they called it, where they'd climb into Bijan's convertible with beach chairs, but no specific destination in mind—following their nose and whims until the inner voice told them to pull over. Discussing anything and everything along the way. What magic.

Rose would bring her sketchbook, of course, and Bijan, his schoolbooks. Over the course of several months, he landed on a title for his thesis—*Catalysts toward Forgiveness: A Case Study of Reconciliation*

Following the Bosnian Genocide. He wanted to explore the psycho-spiritual mechanisms by which the human heart, even following the most evil of transgressions, is able somehow to foster love. Rose, meanwhile, began obsessively drawing him as he pondered and paced on the beach in search of his topic, producing dozens of sketches, which led to numerous canvases—enough, she thought, for a one-woman show. If only she could find a gallery to represent her.

On that particular coastal drive in early January 2018, notebooks and sketchbooks were left in the car. The only thing they'd brought out onto the beach that day was the translated manuscript by Joseph Rakow, which they read aloud to each other in fascination, taking one page each.

"My dad was a revolutionary in his youth," said Bijan, explaining that, while he came from relative privilege, his father was one of the many thousands of students who took to the streets of Tehran in 1978 to depose the shah of Iran, whom the CIA had installed and supported for decades.

MFD at the Simons that night was electric.

Nonstop questions; vigorous opinions; lively debate. Juliette, back at Amherst for the spring semester of her junior year, appeared at her place nonetheless on Lani's iPad (the only device allowed at the table).

"What's a Communist?" Samuel kept asking. "What's a Manifesto?"

Juliette, who had been inspired to dive into some background research, briefed her youngest brother on the basic theories of Karl Marx. He wrote his *Manifesto*, she explained, in the mid-nineteenth century—proclaiming how workers should have a right to own the fruits of their labor, and how, when truly united, the collective might of the labor force can bring down tyrants and despots, even the tsar of Russia, regardless of their stranglehold on power…

"Cool! So, Great-Grandpa Joe was a part of that?" Samuel raised his eyebrows in wonder. "He was also a bar mitzvah, like Joe," said Lani, turning to Samuel's older brother.

"But it's not really fair," Joseph complained. "He started learning Hebrew when he was six!" "At least your rabbi doesn't beat the crap out of you," Rose pointed out.

John was only half-listening to his family's spirited conversation. It's not that he was any less invested in his ancestor's travails. He'd known that Joseph Rakow, who died many years before John had been born, had harbored socialist political views. But John had no idea that he was a full-blown revolutionary—this was fascinating. *Is that why I'm such a bleeding heart?* John wondered. Was there a genetic component to our most deeply held political beliefs? Or had those politics been handed down by his mother, Saralie? And this raised another question—what was her role in all of this?

Why had the manuscript been buried for all these years? You'd think it would have held a place of honor on the family bookshelf. Were there secrets in the book? Who had hidden it away? Was it his mother? Or had it been *her* mother, Rose—the family matriarch, after whom his daughter had been named?

These questions and more had been swimming through John's mind for days. But now his thoughts were elsewhere—in campaignland, where hostile actors online had begun trolling his client, Patti Alvarado, which was actually a good sign. It meant people were starting to take her seriously.

Yet it was the content of their smears that had him wondering. They were calling her a "socialist" in memes that included a hammer and sickle, the symbol of the Russian Revolution. President Obama had been called worse during his presidency, so it wasn't terribly surprising. It could be Russian hackers, of course, grabbing at the lowest hanging fruit. But John couldn't help marveling at the uncanny coincidence: no sooner had he discovered that his grandfather may have been involved in the Russian Revolution than the campaign he was advising got tarnished with the same brush. Could there be a connection? Did the malicious actors somehow find out about his past?

While that seemed like a stretch, John himself had been featured in some of these posts, which gave him pause—he'd been keeping a fairly low profile in terms of associating himself with the campaign. That was one of the conditions he'd stipulated after discussing the race with his wife, as he did with all new client relationships. Keep a low profile on this one, Lani had counseled—work behind the scenes (lest it turn into another pro-bono disaster). Here they were, barely into the opening lap—and they were already calling his client a "Commie Revolutionary," like his Grandpa Joe ... who ended up in jail, apparently. *Exiled in Siberia* was the title of the memoir, after all.

John was dying to know the who, what, where, and how of it all. He turned to Juliette on the iPad screen: "When do we get the next installment?"

"He's practically blind, Dad," said Juliette.

While curiosity about their Russian ancestor was percolating in all of the Simons, for Juliette the tingling had been almost cellular. Her body lit up with a sense of sudden purpose, and she found herself trotting daily to Frost library, where she'd spend hours in the stacks, perusing books on Russian history. A librarian had told her about the *Yiddish Book Center Museum*, which happened to be in Amherst at Hampshire College—and that gave her goosebumps. First order of business after they'd uncovered the manuscript had been to locate someone who might be able to translate it.

Grandma Saralie had tried to read the first few pages to them, but her Yiddish was limited. They needed a scholar, and Juliette found the perfect candidate at the *Yiddish Book Center*: Hershl Rabinowitz, an elderly Ashkenazi Jew who had immigrated to America from Kyiv in the early 1940s, just before Nazi tanks rolled through Ukraine in their invasion of the Soviet Union. Hershl was a jolly fellow, always laughing, often humming, but, sadly, with eyesight as poor as a mole. When Juliette had first presented him with the precious family relic several weeks prior, Hershl giggled with delight, cracked his bony knuckles, and began humming, as he dug into his desk drawer to produce a magnifying glass that was so large it bordered on the comical. He stroked his silver beard and began to read aloud, very slowly but with great precision. Juliette very nearly gasped as she began to hear the first words in the story of her great-grandparent, and several weeks later she was practically sprinting back to the *Yiddish Book Center Museum.* Hershl had said that he'd translate one chapter at a time and it would take him a few weeks to do so. It was now time for the next chapter.

CHAPTER 4

FIRST ARREST

My first arrest came in 1903 when I was fifteen on Brisk Street as I strolled with my friend Shaye Yosl, who was also taken into custody. The soldiers provided no reason for our arrest—they rarely did. We were suspected of being revolutionary sympathizers, and that was more than enough.

We were escorted to the police station, where Officer Bondarsczyk, who was known for his cruelty, immediately delivered a murderous beating. He swung at us viciously with his nightstick. I held up my hands in a vain attempt to protect my face, but it proved useless against the determination of this sadist. My ears were ringing and stars flashed in my blurred vision from the relentless pounding of his truncheon.

After Officer Bondarsczyk had bloodied the two of us, the door to the headquarters opened and we were told to enter a hall where two rows of guarding soldiers stood on either side with their truncheons at the ready— this was the gauntlet we were expected to pass through. As soon as we stepped forward the soldiers fell upon us, beating us. I managed to escape from their sadistic paws and to join a group of other arrested revolutionaries who stood among the beds of this police barrack. It was bitterly worse for my comrade, Shaye. He was not able to tear himself from the soldiers' hands, and they beat him so badly that he might have quickly fallen senseless. But when they saw that my comrade was about to collapse they let him go and brought him a pan of water, ordering him to wash up so that there might not be any signs of blood.

Officer Bondarsczyk, his work done, went off calmly to his iron bed, where his bloodied hands groped underneath for a box from which he took a bottle of whisky, which he placed between his dog-like teeth, pouring half a quart of whisky in a single breath into his alcoholic's throat. Having become half-drunk, he threw poisonous glances at the arrestees, seeking a new victim upon whom to pour his brutal rage.

Panic gripped my body. But he found a different victim: Khatskl, the tailor. The wild policeman quickly grabbed the poor fellow by the hair, threw him to the ground, and began to slug and stomp him with his hands and feet.

Evening had fallen. Shadows spread across the barracks, and the room grew even more sorrowful. When the clock struck twelve, all the arrestees were led outside. Dead stillness ruled the outdoors. A unit of soldiers, their rifles on their shoulders, surrounded us and marched us with utmost efficiency to the town prison.

I, along with the other arrestees, was placed behind iron bars—for the first time in my life ... but, unfortunately, not the last. The crowding and stifling in the room was unbearable. The small cell was packed with arrested Bundists and other revolutionaries, but there were hardened criminals with us, as well. A single tin lamp burned in a corner of the dirty room, its glass chimney emitting a thick cloud of putrid smoke that made it difficult to catch one's breath. I was wheezing, deeply disheartened and petrified about what would happen next—was I to be executed? Would I ever see my family again?

That was the first time that I crossed the threshold of spiritual and physical pain and experienced the eternal misery of one who has lost his freedom. But there was a silver lining to this anguish.

The cell into which I was placed already held two political prisoners: Comrade Alexander Gurvits, a student at the Warsaw University who had been caught with illegal revolutionary literature, and Comrade Shloyme Tistshik, a well-known Bundist in Pinsk.

I was a revolutionary. But I was a revolutionary by inclination. I knew very little of the revolutionary social, economic, and political ideas. I was certainly not familiar with Marxism. And for that reason, prison, for me, became a school, a kheyder where I began to learn of the various ideas and theories that were advocated by the revolutionary movements.

My teacher was the student Gurvits. Thanks to him, I slowly became oriented in social and political problems and familiar with revolutionary ideas. Every evening Gurvits would sit and teach me, explaining various concepts, helping me to understand them. His profound erudition was remarkable, as was his unusual memory—he could recite whole chapters of Marx's *Das Kapital* by rote and repeat them to me while patiently explaining them with fiery and fanatical conviction. This made my time in prison more bearable. But it was hardly without trauma.

We had serious tensions involving other prisoners. There was in our cell a criminal named Sasha, who had been arrested for theft and condemned to a three-year sentence. He was violent and sadistic like the guards, and he would harass the political prisoners, demanding money and food rations from us. He wouldn't dare harm us during the day, because we stuck together and defended one another. But Sasha would often come up to me with his wild eyes and whisper: "Tonight, I'm going to strangle you in your sleep." I had recurring nightmares of Sasha's filthy hands around my throat, waking up in a cold sweat with a pounding heart. It was torturous.

In retrospect, I realize that criminals like Sasha, and even the guards themselves, were just as desperate and disenfranchised as the revolutionary prisoners; this is what provoked their violent rage. Some had been arrested for stealing a single loaf of bread to feed their starving families. The whole system was corrupt and unjust.

I spent twenty-one days in prison that time. Though freed, I was paroled under police control, which was no small thing in those days. I could be rearrested under the slightest excuse. And my sentence would then be severe.

But, far from discouraging my commitment to the Revolution, my prison time served simply to harden my convictions. The sense of societal injustice was fundamental to my burgeoning identity as a young revolutionary; I needed to understand firsthand the plight of the proletarian laborer. An opportunity came soon enough, when my sister Sonya begged me to cover her shift at the match factory. Her persistent cough had worsened into full-fledged pneumonia, which had her bedridden. But there were no sick days allowed at her job. If you missed a shift, you were fired. That's why she desperately needed my help.

Happy to comply, I placed a kerchief over my head and put on my sister's dress, then filed into the factory with Sonya's friend Minne and the other workers—about three hundred in all, who shuffled inside with crushed souls and lifeless eyes.

Even though Sonya had briefed me in detail about the production line and the duties of her station, where the matches were sorted into their individual boxes, I was shocked at the grueling and deeply inhumane working conditions.

First of all, the heat was sweltering. Midsummer in Pinsk is hot enough, but indoors, with no windows, no ventilation, and steam-powered machines, the situation was unbearable. No breaks were allowed, not even for water or urination.

Many of the workers looked like they were on the verge of passing out from dehydration. If they did, they were simply pulled off the line by the armed guards that patrolled the assembly line. The suffering worker was tossed outside like rubbish and replaced by another only too eager to gain employment, as meager as it was. Workers in this factory were paid less than twenty rubles per month, enough to buy four sacks of potatoes—and nothing more.

Nearly everyone on the production line was coughing from the presence of phosphorous that was required to assemble the match heads. The toxic dust permeated the air, entering the lungs of every worker with each inhalation that they took—clearly the cause of Sonya's pervasive lung problems. Even after a single shift, I thought I was going to die. I couldn't fathom how Sonya was able to work under these conditions, day after day, and I gained a profound understanding of the urgency for workers to unite and revolt against their oppressors.

Max, for his part, became involved in the printing and distribution of Socialist literature and pamphlets, which put him in precarious danger of arrest on a nightly basis. After working long hours as Father's apprentice, which was critical for our family income, Max would sneak out and go door-to-door with his stack of flyers.

Someone must have tipped off the police about Max's activities, for armed guards came to our house one day and conducted a thorough search of the premises, overturning drawers, breaking apart furniture to look for hidden chambers, emptying cupboards, and smashing plates. My stoic mother was trying to keep it together, but I could see the tears welling in her eyes, as she watched our home—the modest sanctuary that we still possessed—callously destroyed by the police, while we sat helplessly, held at gunpoint around our small table. I exchanged anxious glances with my father, who was clearly agitated, and Max, who seemed strangely calm. He was convinced, apparently, that they wouldn't find anything, for he had buried his cache of literature away from the house.

But then a policeman marched up to us carrying a jacket; I saw Max's face blanch suddenly as the officer drew a Socialist pamphlet from the inside pocket.

"Who does this jacket belong to?" demanded the officer. My father's expression turned to terror; losing Max as his assistant would be disastrous for the entire household. We were already deeply in debt and teetering into bankruptcy, for which they could arrest us all—any loss of income at this point would have pushed us over the edge.

"Answer the question," repeated the officer impatiently. "Whose jacket is this?"

Seeing the panic in my noble father's eyes, I raised my hand suddenly, and, to the shock of everyone, I said, "It's mine."

I knew that I would pay dearly because I was under police parole, but at that moment I gave it no thought. I was concerned only about my family and my father, who could not dare lose my brother. Not even for a single day.

I expected that I would be immediately arrested and would face serious consequences, but to my great amazement the police left the house, leaving me free.

The reason for this unexpected goodwill by the police was that the sergeant who discovered the jacket happened to be a neighbor of ours, living on the same street. He must have felt some remorse at how his fellow officers had destroyed our home, leaving it like a war zone. So he looked my parents in the eyes and said that the police would be back the following day to arrest me—meaning, unspoken but unambiguous, have your son run for his life!

My mother pulled me close after the police left and rocked me in her arms: "My kindela, my kindela," she said, again and again, knowing that we were about to be separated for a long time—how long, no one knew. (Far longer—it would turn out—than anyone expected.)

Sonya dug through the piles of our belongings that had been scattered everywhere by the police and found her head scarf and the one dress that she owned—the same outfit I had used to infiltrate the factory in her stead.

"They'll be looking for a boy," she reasoned. "He'll be safer this way."

Everyone thought it was a clever idea, and I quickly dressed up in my sister's clothing. Father gathered up a handful of rubles and pushed them into my hands. Max grabbed me by my shoulders and pulled me close.

"You're braver than any of us," said Max, in profound gratitude.

"Go to the station," said Father. "Hurry!"

Little did I know, I was never to see him again...

Chapter 5

Keep Your Enemy Close

"Last I heard … they still called it 'The American Dream.' Am I right?"

"Hell, yes—you're right!" Six thousand voices—give or take. In perfect unison.

"It sure ain't called 'The *Guatemalan* Dream.'"

"Hell, no—it ain't!" Right there with him, right on cue.

"I don't believe there's such a thing as 'The *Honduran* Dream.'"

"Hell, no, there ain't!"

"Is there a goddamn '*Costa Rican* Dream?'"

"Hell, no, there ain't!"

"And there sure as shit ain't no lousy '*Mexican* Dream!'"

"Hell, no, there ain't!!"

"There's only one 'Dream,'" boomed Ralph Trent from his podium. "It's called *'The American Dream!'*"

The applause was like thunder. Nonstop for three minutes. John actually snuck out his phone to time the ovation. He was smack dab in the middle of a Ralph Trent rally.

Taking a page from his grandfather's playbook, John had donned a disguise to blend in unnoticed—a pair of work boots he grabbed at

Goodwill, jeans, plaid shirt, leather belt with a Star of Texas buckle, and a MAGA hat to top it off. John could almost feel the hot red hat searing his scalp, which he gave a bit of an itch as he moved farther into the crowd.

Would he have done it without having read about his grandfather's adventures? Probably not. Joseph Rakow's story was starting to seep into their bones—everyone in the family. No sooner had John put down the last chapter than he decided to disguise himself and venture into the lion's den—like Joseph had, to witness the horrendous conditions at the match factory, and later to slip out of town.

John had been hearing about Ralph Trent's latest "American Dream" stump speech, and he wanted to see it with his own eyes—to learn from the *enemy*, as it were. It was illuminating. Trent's base had been galvanized by their candidate's new messaging, for it allowed them the feeling of taking back their own narrative—a narrative that, Trent suggested, was in danger of being usurped by the "immigrant tide"—or tsunami, if the left-wing politicians had their way. As campaign narratives went, it was brilliant.

John wondered if Trent had hired a new communications team—good news, again, because it meant they were feeling a need to play a chess move against the possibility of Patti Alvarado gaining traction. But it was deeply disconcerting that Ralph Trent, who was already polling in the midsixties, seemed to be gaining strength now—by usurping *The American Dream*, no less.

"Extend a goddamn olive branch? Who came up with that crap??" Mark Dunham charged into the office in an apoplectic rage, having stumbled upon something he wasn't supposed to see. He was practically foaming at the mouth. Lani Simon, John's wife, knew enough to keep calm and let her boss blow his gaskets, rather than resist the tantrum, or, G-d forbid—push back.

This was simply another instance of his legendary vitriolic temper that erupted periodically—the Mr. Hyde aspect of Dunham's personality. Most of the time Mark was pure charm, and quite brilliant, which is how he became a founding partner of Dunham & Grilley, one of Los Angeles's premiere advertising agencies—a boutique shop, about forty-five employees—running national campaigns for major brands: apparel, lifestyle, and restaurants, which was Lani's beat. She enjoyed a rarefied position as a part-time creative director. Plus, there was the perk of all perks: the position allowed Lani to spend more time with her family—a dream job if there ever was one, which is why she put up with Mark's paroxysms.

Lani was great at running teams—keeping people motivated and on task, while staying in their lanes—a talent that came with the territory of being the mother of four spirited kids. She was also an original and out-of-the-box thinker, leading to the creative duties, which fell into her lap just over a year ago when Mark's partner, Dan Grilley, got into a serious automobile crash. Lani took over all of the Dunham/Grilley restaurant accounts, including Olive Garden, which came to the firm for a comprehensive rebrand of their image.

Lani and her team had only been at it for a couple of weeks on the Olive Garden makeover—not ready yet to present ideas. Yet, to foster original thinking, Lani had instituted something she called "garbage time"—which meant any concept, no matter how absurd, was worthy of exploration. She divided her twelve staffers into four groups of three—for freeform brainstorming sessions. One group had been using the conference room, and they'd written their "garbage" ideas on the whiteboard, which is what Mark Dunham had stumbled upon and despised. So much so that he insisted Lani march her entire team into the room for an explanation.

He pointed in derision at the slogans and loglines that had been scrawled across the whiteboard. "This is abominable," he barked. "And I want to know who's responsible for it."

The basic idea—hardly without merit, thought Lani—was that Olive Garden was a sanctuary where one could "extend an olive branch," meaning:

Make Peace With:
A Jilted Lover A Hurt Relative An Angry Boss

It must have been that last line that was sending Dunham into a tizzy, and Lani had a pretty good idea of who came up with it—the new intern, Melody, who was quite bright, and also on the autism spectrum. While she occasionally came across some boundary issues and some "inappropriate" behavior, Melody was a great kid, and Lani could see she was terrified of being fired.

"Who the fuck came up with that crap?" growled Mark.

Silence. Heads were about to roll.

"It was me," said Lani—pulling a Joseph Rakow, just like John had, donning a disguise to learn from the enemy.

Mark glared at Lani, who shrugged it off. "We were just messing around," she tried to minimize the situation. "What? You can't take a joke?"

"It's fucking stupid," said Mark, storming out of the room.

Lani exchanged a glance with Melody, who looked relieved and very grateful to have been spared the wrath of Mark Dunham. Lani was proud of herself for having taken a stance against her egotistical boss; she also felt her share of gratitude—toward her newly discovered grandfather-in-law, Joseph Rakow, and his extraordinary story.

Lani was amazed and delighted that, on some level, she, too, had taken inspiration from his hundred-year-old Yiddish journal, like John and the kids.

She also had an epiphany about an act of courage.

It can be quite lonely.

CHAPTER 6

EXILE

I'll never forget the gripping feeling of isolation that seized me as I stole through the alleys of Pinsk on my way to the train depot. I was on my own. Going where? I had no clue. But surely a place where I'd be a stranger—with no one but myself to lean on.

I was barely fifteen. I missed my mother already.

With only a handful of rubles, I couldn't afford a proper train ticket but had to wait instead in the field beyond the platform to board a westbound train on the run, as it rumbled out of the station. Though I had seen vagabonds do this before, it proved devilishly difficult to secure a handhold as the train built up speed. I scraped my forearm and knee on some sharp metal as I climbed up to the roof of the rearmost car.

From this perch atop the train, I could see for miles. The westbound track pointed like a glistening arrow toward the setting sun, which painted the sky in flaming stripes. The sight was quite majestic—but I was in no mood to appreciate its beauty. All I felt was the lump at my throat.

It must have been midnight or so when I became aware of the train slowing down.

There was a cluster of buildings up ahead—the frontier, I assumed. I decided to climb down the ladder and leap off before we arrived, lest gendarmes were patrolling the station. It was pitch-dark. I landed in a patch of brambles, which tore my clothes and left me bleeding. I darted off into the nearby woods—black and dense with growth. As I marched deeper into the thicket to distance myself from the checkpoint, an owl hooted loudly from a branch right above my head—I was startled.

Fear has a way of feeding itself and escalating wildly—especially when one is alone. I began to think that a pack of wolves would emerge and overwhelm me. My imagination conjured up fantastical visions of wild beasts and malevolent specters, lurking in the shadows. I grabbed a stick and clutched it, prepared to fight for my life.

Then I heard voices. Was it my imagination? No, these voices were as clear as day and getting louder. I froze, but my heart was pounding so forcefully in my chest I thought surely they would hear it. To my despair, I was surrounded by a group of men—not gendarmes, thankfully, but a gang of smugglers, who took pity on me. I can't tell you the immense feeling of relief that flooded over me—and gratitude that I would live to see another day. With help from these smugglers, I stole across the Russian-Austrian border at Radziwill, and by morning I was in the city of Brod [Brody, in modern-day Poland].

I was famished, but I didn't want to spend the little money that I had on food, so I grabbed a few apples from a tree on the edge of town and devoured them—this was to be the only food I had for that entire day. Things were lively then in Brod, with hundreds of Russian refugees fleeing tsarist oppression, like myself, in hopes of going on to England or America. The Austrian constables of Emperor Franz Joseph were quite sympathetic and largely left us alone. They had little cause for concern because we were transients, with no intention of remaining in the city. In fact, I soon left myself after hearing of a job opportunity twenty miles away in the Galician village of Holyadov, populated by Ruthenians. Hitching a ride on the back of a farmer's cart, I found work there on an estate—as a mason.

Working with my father, I'd mostly been a carpenter, but I pretended to have experience in all aspects of construction and was immediately assigned to liming the walls of rooms. So I limed … to the best of my ability—and my work was accepted. I worked with all my strength to succeed: overtime, extra hours, whatever it might take to please the employers. I labored there three weeks in a row. And then it was over.

At the suggestion of one of the other migrant construction workers—a Polish Jew, a few years older than myself and just as lonely—I decided to head toward Oswiecim in Austrian Galicia. The journey was three hours by train, for which this time I proudly paid two gulden to obtain a proper ticket with money I had earned.

Carrying nothing but a small linen sack that contained all my possessions (which amounted to a few pairs of underwear), I was quickly cornered upon my arrival on the platform by an Oswiecim gendarme. I panicked thinking that I was somehow back in Russia, where I would be brought to a hearing and thrown behind bars. In my disorientation, I could not understand why the gendarme had approached me. Apparently, he could tell from my clothing that I was a transient, and he was instructing me to stay on the train if I wanted to continue to Germany.

At the same time, the Austrian conductor of the train that had brought me here came up and advised me that it would be better to remain in Oswiecim than to travel farther. I followed his advice and remained in the land of Franz Josef. While the anti-Semitic fervor that would soon sweep across Europe had not yet taken hold, things were marginally better in Austria than they were in Germany.

It was raining when I left the station and went into the shtetl. Two rows of trees flanked the street, which was covered in thick, sticky mud. Walking in the pouring rain, wet, soaked to the bone, I entered the Jewish Galician shtetl of Oswiecim.

Taking shelter in an inexpensive boarding house, I was lucky to find work in a few days. Learning again on the job, I became a tinsmith and tarred several roofs in the shtetl. After working there for a month, however, the tar and the burning sun caused injury to my hands—splitting the skin into painful wounds. I had no option but to leave that work and to seek something different to do.

By then, peysakh (Passover) had arrived. This was in the spring of 1903. Feeling homesick, I decided to return to Brod, where my exile had begun.

When I arrived at Brod it was the evening of the first seder (festive Passover meal).

Jews strolled past me on their way home from shul (synagogue). They walked home in great joy to conduct the seder ... But where was I to go? I went to the home of the man who had told me of the work opportunity on the estate in Holyadov. His name was Mordkhe (Mordecai) Radziviler, and he received me with a hearty sholem aleykhem (welcome), but not a seder meal. Instead, I was directed to the Jewish People's Kitchen, where I encountered other stragglers like myself. For two ranish [value unknown—trans.], I was able to purchase a meal card for the entire week. While it was nice to share matzah with others and take turns reading from the Haggadah, it made me long for my family and reminded me of how desperately lonely I felt.

During this second stay in Brod, I visited the clubroom of the Polish Socialist Party. I was amazed at how the party members assembled peacefully and calmly, without fear, debating their issues. I had not imagined that somewhere in the world there might be a corner in which a Socialist Party would be legal. I was truly envious of these Brod Socialists.

The Comrades of the club welcomed me, and the Jewish Socialists gave me pamphlets to read in Yiddish. I threw myself into the reading like a hungry wolf. It might have been Karl Marx, or Engels, or Lassalle—I read everything and regarded it all with great respect as containing significant secrets, profound knowledge, and huge discoveries.

When the First of May arrived, I decided to celebrate the (international labor) holiday along with Brod's workers. The celebration was to have been a festive one. A special speaker came from Vienna. The small hall where the Jewish workers gathered was overfilled. When the speaker concluded his "sermon," condemning the terrible exploitation in the feather factories of Brod, where mostly women were employed, the crowd stood and sang "The Internationale."

Far from feeling jubilation and solidarity, however, I began unexpectedly to weep, for this song reminded me of my sister, Sonya, and my brother,
Max—whom I missed desperately. My sobbing became so pronounced that
people began to stare at me, and I had to leave the hall.

I ran into the streets, feeling aimless and sorry for myself. Finding an
out-of-the-way corner where I could sit down in solitude, I hugged my knees
in an attempt to comfort myself. I could not stop crying. Two men came over
to me to see what was the matter with me—their presence was like a little gift
from heaven. It was the farmers on whose cart I had hitched a ride several
months earlier on the way to the estate in the Galician village of Holyadov
(where I had learned to lime walls). They were two Jewish brothers who had
leased a plot of land to plant vegetables. After lending me a handkerchief to
wipe away my tears, they offered me a job. I was hired to guard their garden.

The garden was located several miles outside of town on a broad road
that was flanked by thickly planted pine trees. Across the road, there were
two brick factories. The brothers explained that factory workers had been
stealing their produce and pieces of fruit from their orchard, which is why
they needed a guard to live full-time on the land. I completely understood
the requirements of the job but I also felt slightly guilty, for I, too, in my
many months of exile, had often helped myself to fruit and vegetables from
an unattended garden.

With the help of another employee, a Christian, I patched together a
wooden booth that was to be my lodging. The tenant farmers provided me
with a revolver and a cardboard box containing fifty bullets. They asked me
if I knew how to shoot, and I lied. This was actually the first time I had held
a gun.

"Just a precaution," said the elder of the two, named Max, coinciden-
tally, like my brother. "You shouldn't have any trouble," said the younger,
whose name was Haim. With this, they took off in their cart to their cottage,
which was several miles down the road.

I remained alone on the broad cultivated field. Most of the crops had
been planted recently, so there was little to do other than periodic irrigation
from the well. They had left me several loaves of bread and a large block of

cheese; I was also allowed to eat the abundant strawberries from the garden, along with cherries that were just beginning to ripen. So food was plentiful, responsibilities were few—and idleness, I soon realized, proved precarious. At my other jobs, I had labored continuously from first light until long after dark, whereupon I hit my mattress hard and fell asleep within minutes. Here, I had time on my hands—time to think of my predicament.

I was soon overtaken by homesickness, yearning for my family, my shtetl, and my friends. I strolled back and forth across the broad planted field, terribly beset by loneliness and yearning. It was somewhat bearable by day, but when evening arrived and the skies were lit by millions of stars and dead silence reigned all around, yearning enveloped me and depressed thoughts would not leave my mind.

Sitting thus one evening, wanting to stifle the surrounding dead stillness, I took out my revolver and began shooting into the air. The sounds of the shooting and its flashes and smoke brought a visitor to me that night— an Austrian police official came up and began to interrogate me about the shooting that had occurred. I replied that I had spotted thieves and shot into the air to frighten them and drive them off.

"Be careful with the revolver, young fellow," the official warned me, listening to my tale with a smile underneath his curled moustache, and, with his accompanying dog, he disappeared into the night's darkness.

Several weeks later, when the rows in the field were covered in green cucumbers, the tenant farmers hired a score of Polish women to harvest the vegetables. My employers assigned me to two tasks: in addition to making sure that the harvested greens were not taken, I also had to wash the cucumbers and pack them into sacks.

Pleased to have chores again that kept me busy, I worked well, and after a day's labor I would turn into my booth and the entire prosaic world would vanish from before my eyes...

Asleep in my booth, I heard what I thought was someone knocking at the door one morning. Still half-asleep, I imagined these were thieves or robbers. So I stuck my hand through the little window and fired off two shots into the air.

My revolver had become a plaything with which to pass the time. In the frequent moments when I felt overwhelmed by loneliness, I would take it out and shoot. In that way I had foolishly fired all the bullets that my boss had left me—which meant I would be vulnerable should a situation of real danger arise. And that situation came soon enough.

A band of smugglers descended upon the little farm. Like the gang who'd helped me cross from Radziwill to Brod in my escape from Russia, these four men (and one woman) earned money by sneaking goods back and forth across the Russian border. Laughing, in good spirits, they meant me no harm. The woman was trudging like a clown in a pair of oversize shoes through the mud in between the rows of lettuce that I had just watered. She looked at me with a comical grin. One of the men explained that they had acquired a shipment of new shoes that they wanted to smear with dirt so that they would appear to be used and they would not have to pay customs duty on them at the border.

Thinking my gun was empty, I decided to have some fun. I drew out my revolver and, aiming it at the woman frolicking in the mud, I suddenly pulled the trigger. The woman was terrified—as you can imagine. To calm her, I pointed the gun at my own temple and pulled the trigger again.

In the distraction of my colorful guests and my own foolishness, I had not heard the cart pulling up behind me with my two bosses, who were rightfully perturbed. The smugglers darted off suddenly with their stolen shoes, as my primary boss (Max) marched up to me with a frown. Seeing how casually I was playing with the revolver, he snatched it from my hand and examined it. Then he turned the revolver aside and pulled the trigger. A terrible bang sounded. The revolver had fired.

In his great anger, he slapped me. I accepted the slap in good grace because I felt that I might have killed either the woman or myself. And this so upset me that I could no longer abide remaining on that field and, generally, remaining in a foreign land. I no longer cared that a major punishment awaited me in Pinsk. It was time to go home.

Chapter 7

Where the Heart Is

Soulful … melancholy … longing.

Twelve-year-old Joseph Simon could certainly relate to the emotions that had been haunting his great-grandfather, Joseph Rakow, the man after whom he'd been named. He'd been experiencing a flood of those moods himself.

It concerned a girl. Her name was Eva Golden.

Every time he caught a glimpse of her, Joseph felt awash with feelings that were both exhilarating and terrifying. But he had a sense of what was happening to him. Joseph remembered that time in first grade when he'd caught his sister, Juliette, who was fourteen at the time, weeping in bed with her journal while listening to the classic song "You're My Best Friend" by Queen.

Having stayed home from school claiming to be sick (heartsick was more likely), Juliette thought she was alone in the house, when Joseph came home unexpectedly and peered in through the crack in her bedroom door. He could see Juliette, clutching her yearbook and singing at the top of her lungs to an open page with a picture of her heartthrob.

His name was Hunter Spaulding, the high school basketball star and senior voted "Most Likely to Break Hearts"—which was clearly happening already.

Little Joseph thought his sister's adulation of Hunter was hysterically funny at the time, so he barged into the bedroom cackling like a demon, which mortified Juliette. She slammed her yearbook, shut the music off, and didn't speak to her brother for two weeks.

It was Juliette's first crush—something she was deeply private about, and something that Joseph, at the time, could not begin to fathom. Now, six years later, he was gripped in the same thrall.

How had it snuck up on him with such stealth and speed?

It seemed like only yesterday that Joseph and his buddies were rolling their eyes at girls—making fun of their drama and obsessions. But the teasing had changed in tenor between fifth and sixth grade. It had an entirely new motive: they actually wanted the girls' attention. And the girls were often happy to oblige, which led to furtive stares and secret smiles.

Then came the lightning bolt: The day that Eva Golden, with her liquid eyes and amber hair, looked at him and said, "I think we have the same Parsha."

Joseph's heart skipped a beat, as he took in this life-changing information. Their birthdays, it turned out, were just three days apart. "We're going to be sharing the Bimah," smiled Eva.

As was often the case at their synagogue, Rabbi Weiss had made the decision to hold a girl's bat mitzvah and a boy's bar mitzvah on the same day, meaning the two of them—a B'nai Mitzvah on November 3, which was now less than seven months away—would be leading the service together.

Joseph felt himself being pulled simultaneously in two directions. This was, at once, the miracle of all miracles—but it was also a disaster of unparalleled proportions. How could he possibly be expected to maintain his composure reading complex Hebrew scripture, and also deliver a cogent interpretation of the text, with Eva Golden within kissing distance?

He'd been obsessing over her for months. Her contagious laugh. The way her long, "golden" hair fell like a waterfall on her soft shoulders. It was as if Eva Golden were heaven-sent—a real-life angel. Indeed, her radiance made it hard for Joseph to even look at her directly. He'd sneak glances at her across the temple when she wasn't looking, Or in English class, where Miss Franco had decided to configure the chairs in a circle to facilitate group discussion. And, as if the pressures of puberty were not enough, Miss Franco had also decided that this was the year to introduce them to romantic verse.

Giggles and whispers rippled throughout the room, as she read the classic lines from Elizabeth Barrett Browning:

How do I love thee? Let me count the ways.
I love thee to the depth and breadth and height
My soul can reach, when feeling out of sight
For the ends of being and ideal grace.
I love thee to the level of every day's
Most quiet need, by sun and candle-light.
I love thee freely, as men strive for right.

The kids were squirming in their seats. "Get over yourselves," said Miss Franco. "Any day now, these words will resonate in your souls like gospel truth."

For Joseph Simon, that was already happening.

…I love thee with the breath,
Smiles, tears, of all my life; and, if God choose,
I shall but love thee better after death.

Eva caught him staring. The speed at which Joseph averted his gaze almost gave him whiplash. His buddy, Eli, having seen what had just transpired between them, dug an elbow into Joseph's ribs and whispered: "You're toast, dude."

Gospel Truth—Joseph Simon was officially toast. At least in the presence of Eva Golden.

"Aren't you excited?" bubbled Eva, refilling her soda next to Joseph in the school cafeteria the following day. "I think our Parsha is juicy! Who can't relate to sibling rivalry?"

Joseph found himself tongue-tied—distracted by his buddies, who were snickering at him from a nearby table. "I think it's so empowering," Eva continued. "To stand up and be able to state the truth of how you feel."

If only she knew, thought Joseph…

In one month's time, they'd be meeting every Wednesday after school with Rabbi Weiss to learn Hebrew side by side. Wow.

And, simultaneously—oy vey.

"They're going to love you," said Bijan, taking Rose's hand and escorting her up the porch stairs of the ranch home that his parents had rented in West Los Angeles. When Bijan had been accepted two years ago to the prestigious graduate program at UCLA, which combined a law degree with a PhD in philosophy, his Iranian parents were elated. He'd been awarded a full scholarship, no less—an amazing accomplishment. But they were also devastated by the news—the thought of Bijan, their only child, being so far away. They had always been extremely tight as a family. So Farshid Yadzani, a professor of literature at the University of Tehran, decided to follow in his son's footsteps by applying for a fellowship at UCLA, which came through with an offer of a residency for Professor Yadzani as a visiting lecturer on Sufi Poetry.

Bijan's mother, Esta, an author and art historian, had had to give up her position at the National Museum but did so gladly in order to follow "the boys" to California, where she fell in love with the ocean and applied for a job as a docent at the Getty Villa, so she could gaze at the glorious Pacific during her breaks. Haze would blur the distinction between water and sky on most days. But every so often, especially in the winter months, the horizon would appear as crisp as the edge of a razor, and stunningly beautiful. On those occasions, Farshid would drive down Sunset Boulevard from his campus office in Westwood to join Esta for lunch. Bijan would sometimes join them, too.

While twenty-somethings are usually eager to leave the nest and distance themselves from their parents, Bijan was thrilled to have his folks with him in La La Land (they'd watched the movie in Tehran by way of "research" before leaving, along with Steve Martin's *L.A. Story* and *Sunset Boulevard*, knowing full well that they were getting an entirely skewed picture of life in Los Angeles, but enjoying themselves nonetheless). Bijan got his own place near campus with two other international students to have some separation, but he spent time with his folks every weekend. Sometimes, they'd go for overnight excursions to explore Big Sur or Joshua Tree and other stunning examples of California's natural beauty.

"Breathtaking," said his mother, after a particularly memorable twilight hike up the Paseo Miramar trail to the revered bench that overlooked both a carpet of city lights and also the Santa Monica Bay.

"Inspiring," added Bijan.

And then his father commented on the fact that both of those words refer to the act of inhalation and how interesting it was that, in moments of transcendence, we often invoke our breath, the mystical rhythm that connects the inner and outer world—and also bookends our human lives.

In moments like these, Bijan felt such love and appreciation for his parents and everything they had given him. His mother, on top of her other accomplishments, was also an incredible cook. And that's why Bijan was so excited to share a home-cooked meal with Rose, who was unfamiliar with Persian cuisine, and slightly anxious about meeting her boyfriend's parents.

But Rose's nerves dissipated the moment that Farshid and Esta greeted them at the door with such warmth, it seemed like she was already part of the family. Rose handed Esta a potted orchid she brought as a gift (Mom's favorite flower, Bijan had told her). Esta's dark eyes sparkled with joy.

"So thoughtful," she gazed at Rose, taking her by the hand. "Come," she said, welcoming Rose inside. "Let's check the *fesenjan*."

As Rose crossed the vestibule, she took in their home and liked it immensely—tasteful artwork on the walls, carefully curated objects in specials nooks, rich tapestries, and Persian rugs. It felt warm and embracing. Esta placed the orchid on the coffee table, alongside some delicious-looking appetizers she had laid out in an artful arrangement.

"Your name figures prominently in Persian cooking," smiled Esta, handing Rose a glass of rose water and leading her into the kitchen, where enticing smells from the stove were wafting through the house like tempting tendrils.

Esta had Rose sample her *fesenjan*, the classic pomegranate walnut stew, an essential part of every Persian wedding. She took delight in explaining that this iconic recipe went back to the time of Alexander the Great. Archeologists had actually discovered inscriptions of its ingredients on stone tablets from the ruins of Persepolis.

"Can you guess the spices?" she asked Rose. "Cinnamon?"

"And...?"

Rose tried another spoonful. She couldn't quite put her finger on it. "Saffron," said Esta. "Not very common in the West."

Farshid entered to scoop their guest away. "My turn!" They were competing playfully for her attention. "Bijan tells us you're an artist. Are you familiar with Persian miniatures?" He led Rose into his study, where several exquisite examples were on display. Rose found it touching just how proud the Yadzanis were of their culture and how excited they were to share it with her.

"Your ancestors—they are Ashkenazi? Or also Sephardim?" he asked curiously.

Interestingly, Rose had been wondering about that herself—were all her Jewish relatives from Northern Europe, or could some of them have hailed from the Middle East, like Bijan? The journey of discovery through the memoir of her great-grandparent had piqued Rose's interest in her genealogy, so she'd picked up a 23andMe kit and sent in a saliva sample. The results would be in soon.

"Both sides of my father's family come from Russia, so we're Ashkenazi, I think," she told Farshid. "But my mom's family comes from the Philippines."

He nodded with a smile. "In the end, we all come from Africa, yes? The Garden of Eden, they say, is in Tanzania."

Dinner began with a bell. It was a Yadzani family ritual—assimilated by way of the Himalayas. Farshid struck a Tibetan singing bowl, and everyone sat in silence until the ring was no longer audible. Rose loved it—an ecumenical, nondenominational, and sonic form of grace.

"It's where we meet, in the end," explained Farshid. "In the stillness that connects all hearts." "Rumi's field," said Bijan.

"Exactly," said his father, one of the world's preeminent scholars of the Sufi mystic's work.

Looking around at the Yadzanis—Bijan and his beautiful parents—Rose's heart felt full of love. This family was so different from her own—different culture, different religion—yet so alike in all the ways that mattered.

She glanced at the rose petals floating in her water glass. And felt at home.

CHAPTER 8

SACRIFICE

The day I left Brod to make my way home was an exceptionally beautiful one, which served to blanket me in a feeling of optimism. The fields were decorated with green; blooming fruits dangled from branches; trees along the boulevard were shimmering with millions of green leaves. Flocks of birds swept across the sky, darting from one place to another. The forest ahead echoed with the sonorous hum of insects.

This is where I hoped to cross the frontier, but without guides to help me I knew I could easily get lost. I ventured nonetheless into the thick woods and almost immediately had a scare—when a wild boar exploded from a thicket and darted past me. I grabbed a large stick to wield as a weapon against future wild animals or other possible assailants. Though it was dim under the tree canopy, I kept my eyes peeled, hoping for an encounter with that same group of smugglers who'd shown me the way through these woods on my escape from Russia.

After walking for an hour, I spotted a figure up ahead and approached him, hoping that he knew his way around this forest. But as I got closer, the man raised a rifle and my heart stopped. He was wearing the uniform of a Russian soldier. I'd been caught.

I quickly came to see, however, that he appeared to be just as nervous as I. He was in his early twenties—and scared, a deserter, fleeing Russia just like I had months earlier. Everyone in my homeland had been growing increasingly apprehensive as our forces mobilized for a massive war with the Japanese Imperial Army—which significantly outgunned and outnumbered us. This poor boy did not want to die.

"Watch yourself," he whispered with wild eyes, as he darted desperately toward the hope of freedom in Austria. "They're coming for us!"

I had heard that desertion was a serious issue within the Russian military, and punishable, therefore, by summary execution. Sure enough, within a few minutes, I encountered a patrol, fanning out across the woods—with guns drawn and ready. Trying not to panic, I dived to the ground behind a fallen log. Did they have dogs? Thankfully, no. By a miracle, they stomped past me, as I held my breath in my hiding place.

I waited until I could no longer hear them, then I ran as fast as my shaking legs could carry me, until I emerged, at last, on the Russian side of the woods. What a relief! I could see the train tracks in the distance. As before, I found a spot to hide alongside the tracks and waited for an eastbound train that would take me back to Pinsk.

Hours later, as I jumped off the train just before it reached the depot, I knew immediately that something was wrong. Cossack guards were everywhere. The town seemed to be in a state of pandemonium. Tensions had escalated dramatically between the tsarist forces and the revolutionaries. I learned later what had caused this.

Apparently, there had been a series of homemade bombs detonated in acts of sabotage against the regime, which was now cracking down and rounding up anyone suspected of having revolutionary sympathies. One of my cousins, I would later learn, was severely disfigured in one of these bomb blasts.

With Cossack guards patrolling in numbers, I decided to wait until nightfall before attempting to cross the city and return to my family. By the time the town clock struck midnight, the streets had quieted down considerably, and I made my way through the back roads to our neighborhood. As I approached the modest home that our father had built for us, I experienced a feeling of warmth flooding over my being. I was beyond ecstatic to be on the verge of a reunion with my siblings and beloved parents, who surely would all be slumbering at this late hour.

My surreptitious arrival was noticed initially only by our small black puppy, Shorek, lying near his hut in the yard. But instead of greeting me in the friendly manner in which he welcomed almost everyone, Shorek lay whimpering and yowling in pain—unable to move. As I approached him, I saw to my horror that the poor puppy was bleeding—it looked like he had been struck by a sword! That's when I knew that something was terribly wrong. I looked around quickly to survey the surrounding area but saw nothing. So I darted over to the window of the room that we all shared as our bedroom to see if I could peer inside. The shutters were wide open—another bad sign.

I scanned the interior. The room was empty—it looked like it had been ransacked. My mind went to dread. What had become of my family? All manner of horrible thoughts raced through my beleaguered brain. I'd been on the move without sleep for thirty-six hours and was nearing collapse. But I didn't feel safe inside the house, so I decided instead to sneak into the small barn where we kept a goat. I was in a state of shock, and my exhausted mind did not register the fact that our goat was gone, too. I curled up in the hay and went out like a candle.

Next thing I knew it was morning and someone was shaking me awake. I gasped, but my fear turned to elation when I realized it was my brother, Max. He was shocked and disturbed to see me.

"G-d, my G-d," he hissed, "why did you come here now? They will surely arrest you…"

Someone walked up behind Max and cuffed him on the head: "What's the matter with you?" (It was my sister Sonya!) "Doesn't he deserve a hug first—before you berate him?" She knelt down and embraced me so tightly that I felt I might suffocate.

After I gave them a quick rundown of my adventures in exile, they explained that the family had been in hiding for weeks. The house was being watched by the security forces. We were all in danger of arrest at any moment. Father decided to sell everything, including the goat, and use the money to pay for forged travel documents so they could flee the country. They were leaving that very day, in fact—the rest of the family was already at the train depot. Sonya and Max had come back to retrieve two important things—Father's heavy winter coat and Mother's jewel box, which they had buried here in the barn. Sonya dug them up at once from under the haystack, for there was no time to waste.

"You should have stayed in the West," exclaimed Max. "We can't take you now." "We'll sneak him onto the train," Sonya argued.

"Not without travel papers," Max snapped. "We won't even make it back to the station. Cossacks are everywhere!"

As much as Sonya tried to make a case for me, she knew, ultimately, that Max was right. Both she and Max were carrying "official" papers—with the stamp of Tsar Nicholas that looked real, even though it had been forged. I had nothing. If we were stopped, the police would likely detain all three of us.

Tears began to flow down my sister's cheeks, as she realized we'd once again be separated. But I accepted the situation. It was the only choice. I was not willing to risk that my family would be caught on my account. Better that I attempt to sneak out on my own, as I had done before. Max grabbed a trinket from the jewel case that Sonya had just retrieved.

"Here," he said. "Take this to Chaim Lescher, the forger. Last house on Brestskiy Lane. He'll fix you up with travel documents."

I glanced at the trinket, doubting its worth. None of my mother's jewelry had much value, most of it second- or thirdhand. One item was special, however—the pearl earrings she'd inherited from her mother. Sonya pulled them out of the box. But she didn't give me both of them—just one.

"Earrings come in pairs," she said. "They must be reunited! Come as quickly as you can," she added, clasping the twin of my earring symbolically in her hand. "We'll be waiting for you."

"Good luck," said Max, pulling me close. Sonya handed me father's winter coat, as well—saying I may need it. She wanted me to have one item from each of my parents, so I could remain feeling connected to them. I hugged my sister, trying not to cry and staying strong so she could leave without adding to the worry that she already was shouldering.

Then we heard noises coming from the yard. As we peered through the cracks in the stall's walls, we saw that the police had surrounded our house!

"Run out the back," I whispered urgently. "If they find you with me, they'll arrest all of us!" My sister hesitated.

"He's right," said Max solemnly. Sonya knew it was true.

"What about you?" she asked apprehensively.

I felt the rise of adrenaline. "I'll create a diversion."

With a final glance between us—conveying unspoken volumes—my siblings went to make their move out the back door—but a terrible surprise awaited us: two policemen were on guard in the neighboring courtyard. We hadn't realized that the entire area was under police guard. Sonya managed to duck behind a barrel and was quietly surveying the scene for possible escape routes. The two cops pulled out their revolvers and pointed them at Max and me—we were separated at opposite corners of the yard.

The cops were panning their guns back and forth as if not knowing which of us posed the greater danger.

"Over here," I shouted at them in Russian, waving my hands in the air. Then I whispered in Yiddish to Max: *Loyfn!* ("Run!")

To draw the attention of both guards, I pushed over the nearby hay cart, which toppled to the ground in a loud clatter. I saw Max sneak off to follow Sonya into the alleyway. My next move was as desperate as it was dangerous. Needing to keep the attention of the guards, I quickly sprinted across the yard and leapt over a fence of tall, pointed wooden boards, fleeing like a whirlwind from the hailstorm of lead bullets that pursued me.

Shots rang out from all directions. The cops began chasing me. I ran with supernatural effort as bullets hailed all around. It was the adrenaline coursing through my veins—that primordial urgency we have to survive no matter what. It had taken me over, as I made sudden decisions to dart in one direction or another. Time expanded and stood very nearly still. I could almost see the bullets as they whizzed past and ricocheted off buildings.

Scrambling and out of breath, I found an alleyway that seemed strangely silent. I felt, by some miracle, that I had escaped my two cops. But suddenly I was faced by a pair of civilian-dressed undercover cops who renewed the gunfire from the opposite direction in a fiery rain.

I felt warm blood running down my body. I had been hit!

Refusing to surrender, I caught my breath and ducked into a courtyard, where I crouched in desperation behind a wooden fence. But the two undercover cops caught me in the blink of an eye. My energy had left me. Blood soaked through my trousers. The first two policemen caught up to us. When they arrived on the scene, seeing that I'd been captured, Officer Dekovitsky, a cold-blooded assassin, shot at me from a few paces away. I raised my arm in horror as the bullet came at me.

The police turned to other business, believing that they had murdered me. But the killers were bitterly surprised. My left arm, raised in front of me, had saved me. The bullet had lodged in the bone of my arm. The bone was shattered.

A commander arrived on the scene and ordered for me to be taken to the hospital.

The cops pulled me to my feet, expecting me to walk. Helplessly, leaning on the arms of my persecutors, I barely managed to drag along. My clothes continued to become soaked with my blood. My feet began to fail me, and my body began to weave.

As I was unable to continue my forced march, the police appropriated the horse cart of Mikhal Katak, the owner of a local tavern. After I was seated in the cart under guard of police, the drayman set off at a fast trot. The cart bounced up and down, causing me excruciating pain as strong streams of blood poured continuously from my left side and bullet-riddled left arm. Although I had lost much blood, I did not lose consciousness.

Upon my arrival at the courtyard of the Pinsk (Jewish) hospital, a large curious crowd awaited me. No longer able to walk, I was placed on a stretcher—the same kind on which they carried the dead. I was taken immediately to the operating room, where I was met by two doctors and sympathetic nurses. The assistant police chief, who had wounded me with the first bullet, stood there in the civilian clothes he had donned.

Officer Dekovitsky, who had shot me in the arm, stood alongside, and both admired the work they had done. Then the killers were sent out of the operating room, and I received medical assistance.

As I was still in shock from the loss of blood and simultaneously feverish from the emotional upheaval, the first order of business was to stabilize and hydrate me, which they did with little ice chips, since I lacked the energy to drink and was experiencing nausea on top of everything else.

It's when I was placed in the hospital bed that I first realized the extent of my painful wounds. Time moved very slowly ... I kept asking what time it was ... it seemed to me that the night would never end ... the ice in the rubber pack would quickly melt on my burning forehead as I lay there only a few hours and it seemed that years had passed...

Hallucinations plagued me. I saw a mounted Cossack regiment holding up their gleaming sabers—on which were impaled a thousand decapitated heads. The tsar stood before them, surrounded by a restless pride of lions and leopards, who roared and yowled as foam ran from their bloodthirsty snouts. In his right hand the tsar held a large flask filled with blood, which he poured over his head like an unholy sacrament.

Then he issued a command ceding all the decapitated heads to his lions and leopards. The tsar called out: "Bring me the head of the last mutineer!" All at once the Cossack horde turned to me and shouted in unison: "The tsar demands your life! You have only a few minutes left to live. Say your last prayer quickly and beg G-d for mercy for the sins you committed against our Little Father Tsar."

"No!" I shouted in desperation. "There is no G-d on this earth! If there was a G-d who saw our suffering, he would send down lightning and all you savage animals would perish along with your Little Father Tsar. No, there is no G-d on this earth."

The Cossacks shot me…

I awoke from the nightmare. Every part of my body was in terrible pain. My head burned. My lips were dry and my skin was peeling from the fever. I felt the weight of a hand on my forehead. The feldsher (paramedic) Nikolai stood over me. He ordered more ice for me to swallow.

It was daybreak. I was finally able to look around the filthy and over-crowded hospital ward. Scores of sick peasants with broad, unruly beards, long hair, and sleep-ridden eyes sat and lay on their beds, smoking cheap shag tobacco in wooden pipes, befouling the air. I felt I was being choked by the horrible odor that engulfed the place. A mentally ill peasant, blind in one eye and missing a hand, ran around the room, singing religious hymns.

A cousin of my father, Beyltshe (Bella), whose husband was in America, had been dismembered by a bomb. When I saw her lying there on an iron cot, it was a terrible sight. Her entire body was swathed in bandages. Her head was, as well. Only two circular holes were cut out for her eyes to see and two more for her nostrils and mouth. My cousin recognized me and tried to move her head to greet me. Her pain was so great that she apparently couldn't even smile.

A friend of our family, Comrade Arn Yudel, whom I had not seen since returning home, came by to pay his respects to Bella. Then he came over to visit me at my cot and stretched out his right hand to greet me. We regarded each other, and I suddenly noticed that his left sleeve was empty: his other arm was gone ∴.. another bomb, no doubt.

My own condition grew worse from day to day. My wounds started to reopen. I began to bleed again … terrible pains … my arm swelled up. Forced to lie on my back, unable to turn over, added to the pain. In addition, I had the unbearable thought that I may never arise from this sickbed, nor see my family again.

My fever had reached above forty degrees Celsius (104° F). The doctors at the hospital were shaking their heads … my spirit then was floating between two worlds … at times I imagined that frigid death would swallow me … And precisely when those sorrowful thoughts about death consumed me, a powerful desire developed in me and I spoke to myself: "I do not want to die alone in this miserable place … I want to live!" I murmured.

"Give me my freedom!" I shouted.

Finally, the following morning, my fever broke. My condition had stabilized, which meant they could now schedule my surgery. When I was brought into the operating room, the chief surgeon, Pantskevitsh, told me that surgery must be performed on my arm and that were I to resist, I would die of fever within a few days. The hospital had apparently run out of anesthetic (or they didn't want to waste their precious ether on a political prisoner). So the doctor signaled his assistants to keep me still. Two hospital aides sat down on my feet; the policemen who guarded my room day and night took hold of my head with their heavy hands. I closed my eyes in terror, as the doctor went to work with his tongs and scalpels.

I imagine that my desperate screams must have echoed through the entire city of Pinsk, but in the midst of screaming everything turned black— and I lost consciousness.

When I awoke, I was back in bed. A rubber ice pack was on my head. Dr. Pantskevitsh had a pleased look on his face—it went well, apparently. I felt as though a heavy weight had been lifted from me. My wounded left arm had grown thinner … but the needle-like piercing had receded, and I breathed more easily.

I began recovering slowly after the operation. In the long weeks of my convalescence, the wounds in my left arm and left side began to heal. When I was able at last to get out of my sickbed, my mind went immediately to thoughts of escape. There were frequent whisperings amongst the political prisoners in the ward of when and how such a plan might be possible. I was desperate to be reunited with my family.

The brothers Khuzhikhofski, who'd been arrested at the Pinsk railroad station with bombs in their hands, now also lay in the Pinsk Hospital. One evening, with the help of a smuggled rope, they descended outdoors from a second-story window and disappeared. The other politicals like myself were envious, for we knew that the Khuzhikhofskis had rescued themselves from long years of hard labor in Siberia…

On July 7, 1903, I was informed that I could leave the hospital. My police guard was then strengthened. This brought tumult to my sickroom. Some ailing peasants in the ward, seeing the police, sat on their sickbeds with fearful eyes and bemoaned my fate. The psychotically ill peasant, Feodor, with his blind eye and sawed-off hand, sat on his iron bed, smiling, as I began to ready myself to leave.

When I put on my clothes, they hung from me as though they had belonged to a much heavier person. I noticed the blood stains on my trousers ... Father's coat had bullet holes in several places. I said farewell to my friends who had come to accompany me as I left the hospital.

In my group of arrestees there was a prisoner named Grisha Drogokupyets, from Yanove. At his arrest he was shot in the leg and now walked leaning on a wooden crutch. Under the open skies, surrounded by an iron perimeter of swords and revolvers, we marched forward with a firm will through the narrow streets. The alleys and surrounding area took on a new appearance in my eyes—the entire town and its people appeared as scenes from a fantasy. I could hardly believe that I was walking freely ... but, of course, I was hardly free.

In a short time I spotted the tall wooden fence of the Pinsk prison. The Romanov (tsarist) government had no direct evidence proving my membership in the Socialist Revolutionary Maximalist party; therefore the Pinsk administration had held me under Statute 21 and an amendment to Codex No. 33—that is, under suspicion of being a political opponent of the tsarist dynasty. My prosecution had been assigned to the general governor of the Minsk Region and then to the Interior Ministry, which had accused me of belonging to a revolutionary organization whose aim was to subvert the ruling tsarist régime by terrorist means. Under those charges, I had been informed by the Gendarme Council master of Pinsk that I would be held in the local prison as soon as I returned to health, meaning now.

When the guards brought me close to the wooden gate of the grim living grave, one of them pulled at the handle of the doorbell. The watchman on the other side of the prison door peered through a small window, and, upon realizing that a new inhabitant was being brought in, he opened the door and, as soon as we had entered, quickly shut and locked it. A new chapter of my life began—the life of a prisoner.

I was led to the office of Chief Overseer Libeshevitsh, who noted my name in his ledgers. He handed me to a prison guard, who took me into a room filled with a varied element of prisoners. Passing through the melancholy corridor, I inhaled a terrible odor. My breath was choked. The tall walls and the ceiling were smoke-covered in soot, and spiderwebs hung thickly in the air, fluttering like tree branches. In some places the walls were covered by green, hairy fuzz. The floor of the long passageway was decorated with dried black mud.

A pitiful scene awaited me when I was placed in my cell. There were thirteen prisoners there, among whom one political arrestee, Pavel Tireshko, was bound by iron chains. The room was very small, less than three arshin (seven feet) wide by five arshin (twelve feet) long. No more than two people should have been housed in that cell, but local officials paid that no mind. Half of the thirteen inmates were sick. Three prisoners suffering from typhus lay beneath the narrow wooden plank shelf. Three more victims of the same disease lay on the ground along the cell walls. Some prisoners sat on the plank shelf, their heads bowed, their faces pale.

Other inmates marched to and fro, casting nervous glances. The heavy breathing and moaning of the ill prisoners caused me awful dread. Without consulting anyone, I demanded of the guard pacing the corridor that I be transferred at once to the political prisoners' cell. The occupants of my dark sepulcher regarded me in wonder. They laughed to themselves with their fearful, melancholy faces.

My protest was ignored. But when my comrades in the political section learned of my dangerous situation, the leader among them, Comrade Gogol, demanded of the warden that I be transferred at once to the political section. The demand, however, was rejected, because the warden did not yet know, he said, of what I stood accused. Comrade Gogol did manage to obtain the right for me to join the political prisoners in walking the yard for three-quarters of an hour that very day.

My meeting with my political comrades on the yard produced immediate friendship and hearty, brotherly love. The joy and sudden hope I experienced in those unforgettable minutes cannot be described. These prisoners were part of the extreme wing of our party (SR Maximalists). Embracing some comrades whom I knew personally, I vowed that instant to join their ranks and become a full-fledged member of the Socialist Revolutionaries. After a few brief moments with these inspiring comrades, I heard the saddest sound one could imagine—the whistle that marked the end to our exercise walk.

Upon returning to my crowded cell, I was met with a hellish scene: one of the prisoners lay dead on the floor, having perished from lack of medical attention. A black, broad beard covered the corpse's wizened, pale face. He was removed unceremoniously on a wooden stretcher, and the guards told me, to my chagrin, to take his position ... on the same floor space of the poisonous cell!

The typhus epidemic had spread among the criminals through the terrible crowding and the rotted, unnourishing food. The corpse and its black beard now occupied a significant part of my thoughts, as I attempted to shut my eyes. I was unable to fall asleep that night. Bedbugs crawled over me and bit at my flesh, and I was worried that one of these parasites would infect me with the deadly typhus bacterium that was afflicting nearly half of the prison population. With harrowing thoughts plaguing my tormented mind, it was almost dawn before I fell asleep.

But my sleep did not last long. When I opened my eyes I saw the prison warden standing there alongside Comrade Gogol of the political cell. The warden reported to me that he had received my papers and that, since he now knew that I was a political prisoner, this permitted me to move to where I belonged—with the political prisoners. A few minutes later I was ensconced in that cell.

The political cell was much more comfortable. There was sufficient room on the shelf and significantly better morale—the reason for which was soon explained to me. For some time now, my comrades had been secretly engaged in a proactive plan to reclaim our lost freedom—by planning a daring escape from this hellish prison. Carrying this plan out had not been a simple task—it had required great coordination and stealth. Their cell contained a brick oven. The prisoners had removed its door and created a tunnel below the oven. The sand that they dug up was carried out surreptitiously and emptied into the toilet room ... after weeks of hard work, the excavation was completed.

They invited me to join their escape, and I rejoiced at my good fortune—not knowing, at the time, that hitching my fate to that of my radical comrades would dramatically and tragically backfire.

The excavation stretched from the oven in Cell Number One to the yard outside, where we planned to use stolen ropes with grappling hooks to climb the perimeter fence. That night, following the lead of Pavel Tyeroshko, the ranking member of our little cell of SR Maximalists, we, one by one, crawled into the cramped tunnel. I would be the last to go and was getting increasingly nervous, knowing that the nighttime sentries would soon be making their rounds.

When I finally entered the tunnel it was pitch black, full of dust and profoundly claustrophobic. I couldn't see a thing. The dust kicked up by the other escapees was so thick I could hardly breathe. I began to cough, and my panic increased, thinking the noise would alert the guards. Comrade Yurewicz, who was ahead of me, was inadvertently kicking dirt in my face. The walls of the tunnels were beginning to give way.

Then a sudden whistle, followed by the sound of shouting and scurrying footsteps: the alarm had been raised! Guards were pouring out of their barracks. The entire prison erupted in cacophony as other prisoners woke up, realizing an escape was underway.

Convicts threw themselves to the doors of the cells to cheer us on. Stools, spoons, and plates began to fly at the doors. Wild roars and screeching from hundreds of mouths filled the air.

Comrade Yurewicz and I scrambled desperately through the last stretch of the tunnel. Then our worst nightmare came to pass—the tunnel collapsed, trapping us and burying us alive.

In the many minutes it took the guards to find us and pull us from the infernal tunnel, I thought I was going to suffocate. It was both with relief and dread that I faced my captors, knowing I would soon be the recipient of a murderous beating.

Prisoners were still screaming and clanging utensils from their cells, as the guards dragged us into the yard and started their assault, kicking with their pointy boots and pounding us mercilessly with the butt of their revolvers. I held up my arms to protect my head and accepted the unspeakable pain, waiting for their vengeance to subside—what choice did I have? But when they struck my still-healing wounds, the pain was so excruciating, I thought I might die.

Three days later, with bruises everywhere, we were brought before an administrative judge. We rejoiced in learning that Pavel Tyeroshko and several of our other comrades had made it through the tunnel, managed to climb the wall, and escaped to freedom. It gave me immense satisfaction to know that the revolutionaries had achieved this small victory. But then it came time for my sentencing.

There was no longer any doubt now that I was now a full-fledged member of the SR Maximalists. The judge could have easily condemned me to death by firing squad for my attempted escape from prison. But, showing some clemency because of my age, he sentenced me instead to ten years exile in Siberia. Ten years! My heart plummeted.

This was the moment that I knew … my innocence was gone forever.

Chapter 9

Black and White

The border between Mexico and the United States runs just shy of two thousand miles. Situated at its eastern extremity—where the Rio Grande spills into the Gulf of Mexico—is the city of Brownsville, Texas, along with its Mexican counterpart: Matamoros, a name that's fitting, given the tensions along the frontier. Matamoros means "killer of Moors," a title given to Spain's patron saint, St. James, in the Middle Ages (from *matar*, "to kill," and *moros*, "Moors"). According to legend, the saint appeared during a pivotal ninth-century battle, emboldening the Spanish king to massacre sixty thousand Saracens. The dubious iconography of the sword-wielding *Santiago Matamoros*—a Christlike white man, astride his all-white horse, rearing up as he slaughters the nonwhite hoards—carried over to the Spanish colonization of the Americas, where he was depicted as a conquistador, a rival force to the local gods, and a protector of Spaniards from the indigenous ("brown") people.

It was here in Matamoros, along this fraught frontier, that Patti Alvarado entered Texas illegally with her infant daughter during the summer of 2004. John Simon thought it was time to play that card—by staging a press conference at the border, in which Patti would lay it all out in graphic detail. They needed the media to start paying attention to the campaign—and this stunt could be just the ticket. Patti would speak candidly about the plight of political and economic refugees, like herself, at the very spot where she had stolen across the border.

Though Brownsville was not within her district, John felt the optics would prove irresistible to the media. He had called all the local outlets, and it looked like they were preparing to send crews. John had also tapped a CNN contact, who was nibbling. Who knows? Patti could just get national press on this one.

They had spent days discussing her speech. "Don't hold back" was John's advice. "Give me the grit, the sweat. I want to feel your adrenaline." He was inspired, again, by the writings of his grandfather—whose gripping descriptions of stealing back and forth across the Russian frontier as a boy of fifteen were jaw-dropping. That's how John felt, anyway. Patti's story, he thought, could have a similar impact on the electorate.

Patti had moved to Matamoros in the early 2000s with her first husband, Jesus. Alexa had just been born, and the young couple was looking for a place where their newborn daughter could have the best opportunities. There were plenty of factory jobs in Matamoros at the *maquiladora* assembly plants that were sprouting like mushrooms. The ratification of the North American Free Trade Agreement (NAFTA) had allowed companies like General Motors, Ford, and Chrysler to save millions by outsourcing the manufacturing of automotive parts to a place where wages ran three dollars a day (as opposed to the thirty dollars an hour they'd have to pay union workers in Detroit).

Both Patti and Jesus found factory jobs and started saving money. Like many migrant workers, they lived in a slum on the outskirts of town, where an elderly matron provided affordable daycare for their daughter. This was only a waystation for them—they had no intention of staying, for it was far too dangerous. Matamoros was home to the infamous Gulf Cartel, which supplied one-third of America's cocaine, along with meth and heroin. To make matters worse, Los Zetas, Mexico's most deadly crime syndicate, was vying for control of the area, along with a rival organization—the brutal MS-13 gang from El Salvador, which preyed upon vulnerable migrants.

One day, while walking home from work, Jesus was accosted by several MS-13 gangbangers with machetes who demanded twenty dollars per week in protection money—nearly the entirety of his factory wages. What could he do? He stalled for time, promising to pay them the following day—then darted suddenly down an alleyway. The trio of thugs raced after him, but Jesus was a faster sprinter; he also knew all of the shortcuts through the shantytown and soon eluded his pursuers.

Jesus was completely out of breath when he approached the shack where he lived with his daughter and Patti, who knew from his blanched face that something was terribly wrong. "We have to leave," he told her, explaining the predicament and immediately going to work, stuffing their belongings into a pair of duffel bags. But where could they go? They hadn't saved nearly enough to hire a *coyote*, a professional people-smuggler, who could escort them across the border. That would cost thousands. Yet staying put was clearly untenable. In fact, they hadn't even finished gathering their scant belongings when the MS-13 thugs came upon them. "Run!" shouted Jesus. And Patti took off with her crying baby.

She didn't look back. But she certainly heard the gunshots.

Adrenaline took over as Patti headed north toward the river, where *coyotes* escorted people across on rafts—a luxury she could not afford. It was dusk when she reached the riverbank, which was overgrown with weeds and vegetation. Patti crouched in the shrubbery and caught her breath, thankful that Alexa seemed to have calmed down. She surveyed the situation—less than a hundred feet across the river, which appeared to be shallow enough with a relatively calm current. *Swimmable?*

Patti had heard plenty of woeful tales of mothers drowning with their children in attempts to cross the Rio Grande. But these could also be stories created by the *coyotes* to drum up business.

Surely there were plenty of success stories, she reasoned—ones that wouldn't necessarily be heard on the Mexican side. Patti steeled herself and stared at the water. It would be nightfall soon. No time for hesitation.

John was on the edge of his seat, hearing his client's riveting story. He could barely wait for Patti to continue. "You made it," he blurted. "Obviously, you made it!"

"Alexa and I made it," nodded Patti somberly. "Jesus gave his life for us."

She took a deep breath, squeezing the hand of the now fifteen-year-old Alexa, who was seated next to her in the campaign van as they rolled down Route 77 from Corpus Christi to Brownsville, where the press conference was scheduled to begin in two hours.

John shook his head in amazement. "It's gonna be one heck of a speech."

Patti nodded. "Can you write it in time?" she asked.

"I'm not writing a thing," said John. "You got this."

If there was anything he had learned from his grandfather, Joseph Rakow—people needed to tell their own stories, especially when it came to harrowing narratives of escape from injustice.

One hour later, they were at an outcropping overlooking the Rio Grande—with the border bridge to Matamoros in the background. It was picture perfect. John was thrilled to see a dozen news crews, including CNN and MSNBC. Patti took her place at the podium, along with Alexa, who flashed her braces at the cameras. Her mother, feeling the pressure of the moment, was not smiling, however. She took a moment to compose herself.

"It's good to be in Brownsville," she began. "I myself am very proud to be brown." John gasped. What a line! Everyone was going to run this.

Indeed, CNN decided to carry the entire speech live. And that caught the attention of incumbent Congressman Ralph Trent, who watched the feed with his team in Washington.

"I think we may have a problem here, boss," said his chief of staff. "No shit," responded Trent in disgust.

It all came down to income inequality—the vast and growing division between the "haves" and "have-nots." That's what fueled Populism; both on the left, and the right.

Juliette Simon had been spending increasing amounts of time in the Amherst library, researching the conditions that led to her great-grandfather's arrest. And she was quite amazed at what she had discovered. There was an astonishing connection between the conditions in Russia and America—both back then, and even now, which was one of the drivers of the increasing polarization in US politics. That Russian/American link, which included France in a geopolitical triangle, went back to the time of the Declaration of Independence.

Both France and Russia had taken inspiration for their respective revolutions from the American revolt against the tyranny of King George III, whose iron-fisted rule was not unlike that of Tsar Nicholas and the king of France. So, just two decades after the American colonies seceded from British Empire, French revolutionaries led King Louis XVI to the guillotine, along with Queen Marie Antoinette, whose infamously clueless (and in reality, fabricated) comment about the poor served to underscore the vast societal inequality that fueled that revolution. When told that the peasants lacked bread, "Let them eat cake" is what she is said to have said, according to Jean-Jacques Rousseau—*brioche* was the actual word he used.

Clearly, Marie Antoinette was totally out of touch with the plight of the poor, just like the Romanov Dynasty in Russia. Peasants in nineteenth-century Russia were "serfs," or indentured servants, tied for life to a specific plot of land. It was a form of slavery, wherein they could be bought and sold by the nobility who controlled the land. Then, at the time of the American Civil War, which eventually ended slavery in the United States, serfdom was finally abolished in Russia. But that created its own set of problems—when these newly emancipated workers had trouble finding jobs that paid a living wage, which is ultimately what led Joseph Rakow to join the revolutionary movement.

Juliette, in her curiosity about his ten-year banishment to Siberia, discovered that the authorities routinely chose exile for political prisoners, rather than execution—fearing that hangings or firing squads might produce martyrs and therefore fuel the fomenting revolution. Russia had this vast and largely uninhabited region in Siberia, which, at five million square miles, was larger than all of the United States. It was hard to reach and bitterly cold, especially in winter. Much better to send these revolutionary agitators to the harsh limbo of Siberia, where, out of sight and out of mind, they'd be likely forgotten. Lenin was exiled to Siberia in 1897 and Stalin in 1903—the same year as Joseph Rakow. The Romanovs and their cronies were intent on maintaining their stranglehold on power at any cost.

At that time, according to Juliette's research, the top 10 percent of Russian society controlled about half the country's wealth. What really intrigued her, however, was that the situation was identical in the United States. This is what prompted her to pick up the phone to share her findings with her father, who was delighted to receive a call from his impassioned and endlessly interesting second daughter.

"After we successfully dispensed with the British royals," she explained excitedly, "we created our own elite dynasties in families like the Rockefellers, Carnegies, and Mellons. But here's where it gets sick, Dad," she continued breathlessly. "The conditions today are exactly where they were a hundred years ago."

Though the Great Depression and World War II intervened somewhat to level the economic playing field, in the last three decades the wealthiest Americans consolidated their holdings so that, once again, the top 10 percent now controlled half the nation's wealth. What fascinated Juliette was that the same was also true of modern Russia, with its oligarchs, who were like the new tsars. That's what Joseph Rakow had been up against—centuries-old societal injustice that suppressed the poor and rewarded the rich. Juliette, who had volunteered for Bernie in 2016, felt very strongly about this issue.

"I've decided to change my major," she declared with newfound conviction.

"Oh," said John. It was the third time for his impetuous daughter.

But there was a fresh power in her voice—one that he had not heard until that moment.

"I'm going to be a journalist," she said with pride.

John took it in. It made total sense for Juliette and played to all of her strengths. "What beat?" he asked.

She didn't even hesitate: "Politics."

CHAPTER 10

SIBERIA

On June 17, 1903, we began our preparations for the long journey to Siberia. I'd been assigned to the village of Klimeno, Angorski Region, Pintshuskin County, Veniseysk State. That's where I would be living out the next ten years of my life—over three thousand miles from Pinsk, the farthest I'd ever been from home. Even more difficult for me to accept was the fact that my family would be even farther, in a destination unknown to me—so I would have difficulty even attempting to imagine where they were.

The sun blazed and flies were everywhere as they called us to the dispatch area.

Our group consisted of the following prisoners: the Kuzhikhovski brothers, Solomon Shraybman, Semyon Mazertshuk, Pavel Tyereshko and me: Yosef Rakov. Because of the terrible typhus epidemic that then gripped all of Russia and its central prisons, we were to be checked by a doctor before boarding the trains.

Dr. Galavtshan examined me, and, finding the wound on my arm to be much improved, he wrote a permission slip allowing me to be sent off on the convoy. The doctor excluded my comrade Solomon Shraybman, however, due to ill health. My young comrade panicked—he did not want to be separated from me. So the medic conceded his request that we be sent off together. Dr. Galavtshan showed us much sympathy, and keeping his fists pressed together, he declared: "Akh, such young children are being shipped off to Siberia!" The warden Kravtshenko made no response. His head bowed, he turned aside his sarcastic, evil visage, staring off into space.

A special detachment of police formed an escort around us as we emerged into the street. Heart beating solemnly, surrounded by glistening swords, I marched forward toward certain physical pain and spiritual suffering. Civilians, sympathetic to the cause, lined the road to bid us farewell as we marched toward the train station. The armed force cut a path for itself through the crowd, and an hour later we were sitting in a rail wagon, surrounded by other despondent prisoners and watchful guards.

The train, like a devil, ran swift as the wind across the fields and over its iron tracks. Thick forests, various brooks, and journeying peasants swept before my eyes as shadows. With my soul sobbing silently, I thought of the homeland of my youth and the dear friends whom I so needed now. The locomotive wheezed awfully ... wheels screeched, wagons shook, and a melancholy loneliness weighed heavily on my heart.

Traveling in this manner, we arrived days later, at the city of Bryansk, where we were forced to disembark the train and proceed on foot. Unable to enter the town via the rail line because the bridge over the Bryansk River had collapsed, the convoy took our party across in boats. We were to sleep that night in the Bryansk jail, where the unfamiliar administration took us into the courtyard. Everyone's belongings were shaken out. I surreptitiously swallowed my mother's pearl, as I had done at every stop to protect it from the hands of thieving guards. When the evil ones had completed their devilish searches, we were led through various dark passageways into a basement cell.

People were packed like herrings in that crowded, damp cellar. Many prisoners sat naked, picking live insects from their filthy underwear, overgrown beards, and straggly hair. I was horrified to see a number of them eating the bugs—that's how fierce was their hunger. A laughing guard pushed me into the nightmarish lockup. As the heavy iron door was bolted behind me, everything before my eyes went dark...

A few hours later, I snapped awake from an exhausted stupor—for the first three blinks of my weary eyes, I had no idea where I was. I heard shouting and the sound of truncheons banging against the metal bars. The guards were rousing us in what felt like the middle of the night. It was well before dawn and pitch-black as they herded us outside, along with dozens of other inmates. A military commander informed us, since the railway had been damaged (*by revolutionary saboteurs?* I wondered), we would be making the next leg of our journey to Siberia on foot—a brutal sixty-five-mile forced march from Bryansk to Orlov. I looked at my Comrade Solomon in deep concern. Still weak from his illness, he gave me a half smile, as if to say don't worry—I'll be all right.

But that was the last time I ever saw him.

A sizable military unit took over as our new column escorts. At the front were several soldiers carrying large torches of rags soaked in gasoline, lighting the way on the dark road. Those whose legs were shackled in iron chains were arranged in rows of six. Behind them was a row of prisoners with shackled wrists. The commander let out a shout for us to move forward, and the convoy started out. Chains clanged ... everyone moved steadfastly: the sound of a hundred marching feet.

The mounted guards moved quickly, and the prisoners were driven like poisoned mice. Woe to him who lagged behind. Beatings by the soldiers' gun butts fell to more than one. Stragglers were tossed into the ditch to be eaten by the wolves who roamed the woods that lined the unpaved road. I looked over my shoulder to look for my Comrade Solomon. But all I saw was dust and tired limbs.

It was well past midnight when we finally reached our destination, and our numbers had thinned considerably. Our convoy entered the courtyard of the Orlov jail, and prisoners in the five-story stone buildings greeted us through their small windows, waving hundreds of white handkerchiefs. The guards aimed their rifles at them and shouted threats. All the visages disappeared from the windows for fear of being assassinated. I later learned that the guards received a reward from the administration for every inmate they killed—the sum, under law, was three rubles. There were cases where prisoners were shot to death for the sole sin of daring to look through the iron bars into the courtyard.

In the Orlov transit cell into which I was placed, hundreds of people sat like ants on a heap of moss. Filth, dirt, and lice plagued ragged, half-naked, overgrown, and both young and old men. My eyes were glazed. By now I was getting used to it.

After three full days in the hellish Orlov prison, in which we awaited additional convoys of prisoners destined for exile in Siberia, we were rounded up and marched to the train depot, where the platform was filled with political exiles bound for life sentences. Bundists, SR, Anarchists, Labor Zionists—people of various secular political attitudes—sharing one ideal in life: to destroy the rule of the tsarist hegemony. Among this group of spirited fighters numbering in the hundreds were dozens of Jewish and Russian women who had been sentenced to exile in Siberia. I gazed at these women with sympathy and admiration. It prompted me for a moment to think of my brave sister, Sonya—imagining her free from oppression in the West, soaring above the clouds like a bird. The thought made me smile. And then I realized how long it had been since my lips had turned upward. That's when I noticed a face reflecting that smile back to me—a girl, my age, or perhaps a few years older. She was very pretty with hazel eyes and long, braided hair; and just as lonely as I, no doubt, and yearning for human contact. Her name, I would later learn, was Comrade Rosa. Life had suddenly become more interesting.

A whistle sounded and we were loaded like cattle into the train cars for the long journey to Samara, which would take a week. I jostled and elbowed my way through the crowd to ensure I'd be in the same car as Comrade Rosa, and thankfully I was successful. There were several political women in the car, and the spiritual mood of the prisoners became jubilant. Each one of us was firmly convinced that his or her suffering was not in vain. The soldiers accompanying us felt instinctively that they were not guarding ordinary criminals. The mystical word *politika* streamed like an electrical current, warming their frozen hearts and illuminating their confused, disciplined souls.

The guards took a roll call as the train began its journey. They needed a list of all the prisoners in each car, along with their assigned destinations and sentences. So we went down the line, one by one. That's when I learned her name: Rosa Mendelsohn. I watched her furtively from across the car as she unflinchingly declared her sentence: twenty years, in the town of Ilansky, in the state of Veniseysk.

My heart fluttered—it was the same state as me. I wondered how far apart our villages were. I thought about her sentence, twice as long as mine, and pondered what she'd been accused of. Her eyes were resolute. No regrets.

When it came time to state my name, I tried to embody the brave conviction I had felt from Comrade Rosa, daring not to look at her as I uttered the words "ten years," which still caused me a painful lump in my throat. The roll call continued down the line to a charismatic figure in his twenties with a distinctive walrus moustache. He refused to stand like everyone else had as he gave his name.

"Stalin, Yosef," he mumbled in defiance.

I had no idea at the time who he was; Stalin had not yet risen to national prominence as one of the leaders of the Russian Revolution. But some of my comrades in the train car seemed to recognize his name, for Stalin had achieved some notoriety as a legendary agitator in Tiflis, the capital of Georgia [present-day Tbilisi], where he'd organized massive strikes and May Day demonstrations, robbing banks to pay for his revolutionary activities. He'd already been arrested numerous times, but the authorities were never able to detain him for long. Stalin was Houdini-like in his ability to escape any situation. He had been sentenced this time to Novaya Uda, an extremely remote hamlet in the Udinsky District of Irkutsk—where the authorities hoped the bitter Siberian isolation could keep him contained. (They were wrong; Stalin would be back agitating in Tiflis within a year.)

When the roll call was completed, we sat in silence for a moment, traveling across empty, desolate fields—wondering about our uncertain futures. Then Comrade Rosa stood up again to speak. I glanced nervously at the guards who were wondering just like I was—what in the world was she doing?

Comrade Rosa cleared her throat, took a breath, and launched into the opening verse of the "Internationale." I grinned in elation. Others joined in, and soon the air was permeated by the singing of our revolutionary anthem. Before long, everyone in our car was on their feet, chanting in unison and with great passion. It was so joyous and uplifting—such a contrast to the bleakness of our predicament. What was remarkable is that some of the guards quietly joined our chorus, too. Despite their jobs, which demanded allegiance to the tsar, they were sympathetic to the revolutionary cause.

I will never forget the fervor and camaraderie that Comrade Rosa had inspired in us. A vivid memory of this moment replayed itself in my imagination over the next days and weeks, and it went a long way to ease the silent boredom of our endless journey, as the train chugged deeper and deeper into the Siberian steppes. I would steal glances at Comrade Rosa from time to time. In my mind, I began to compose an ode to her valor. I would also write imaginary mental letters to my family. Anything to pass those unrelenting hours of travel to the extreme isolation that awaited us.

Finally, after nine days on that bone-rattling train, we arrived at Samara, where we were loaded onto trucks to be driven to the municipal prison. En route to the lockup, we were attacked by a terrible plague—clouds of tiny, biting insects. These devilish predators provided us with quite a fine welcome. Everyone in our group began to scratch at themselves, waving our hands and kicking our feet to no avail. When you killed one, a thousand others came to take its place.

As we approached the prison gates, the flies dissipated, to our great relief. It was at this garrison that we'd be separated into distinct convoys to be delivered to our final destinations. I did everything in my power to stay close to Comrade Rosa, knowing we'd been sentenced to villages in the same region—indeed, we ended up in the same cell, along with two dozen other political prisoners who, exhausted from our journey, collapsed like fallen trees to sleep on the dirt floor. We occupied every inch of floor space—a sea of bodies without even the space to turn on one's side. We'd been shoved at random by guards into the cramped lockup, so Comrade Rosa and I were now separated. She was on the other side of the cell, and I glanced in her direction to smile: "Good night." She smiled back. Then, to my astonishment and delight, she clambered across half-a-dozen bodies to sleep at my side. I felt strongly attracted to this brave comrade who, in her short time in our group, had brought so much life and courage into the ranks of our suffering souls—and was now curling up next to me! I began to pepper her with questions about her past and her arrest—but she put a finger to my lips and sweetly whispered: "Shhh."

With that, she closed her eyes and, within seconds, was slumbering peacefully.

I, on the other hand, found myself absolutely unable to fall asleep. I felt Comrade Rosa's moving breasts and breathing quite close to me. When I made a slight movement of my arms, Comrade Rosa's head, with its golden hair, ended up lying on my wounded arm. I was very uncomfortable. My not fully healed arm could not abide the weight of her precious head, light though it was.

I remained horizontal—attempting to feign sleep. But to my dismay, I could not relax. Lying motionless for an undetermined time, I finally decided to try and free my arm. Careful not to awaken Comrade Rosa, who by then was snoring loudly, I slowly pulled my left arm to the right. But that prompted Comrade Rosa's head to roll onto my chest. I lay there stretched out, still and calm. I feared making a move lest Comrade Rosa wake up and I'd be guilty of disturbing the sweet movement of her beating heart. The whole lockup, Siberia's angry nature, and the insects that had so severely bitten us earlier that day, all disappeared for me in a cloud of rapture as my breathing began to fall into rhythm with hers. A new world of aspiring souls and courageous spirits now rose before my eyes. I wanted to hug and kiss the sun and the earth.

Floating amid a fantastical world, I finally fell into a deep sleep. I dreamt that Comrade Rosa and I found ourselves in a field decorated with millions of blooming flowers. Tall mountains arose, thick with conifers, whose resinous odor spread over the entire area. We ran together about the fields, leaping over mountains and admiring the majesty of nature. The wind tousled her long, blond hair, which was now interwoven with red flowers. Her fiery, glowing eyes threw beams into the air.

Then Comrade Rosa was abruptly pulled away from me. She appeared at a great distance, deep into the field. As I ran in sudden panic to reconnect with her, I fell unexpectedly into a terrible swamp, which swallowed me up. Despite my desperate attempts to grasp at rotting branches, I sank deeper and deeper into the abyss.

"Oy!" a heavy sigh emerged from my chest. "I am lost!"

When I opened my sleepy eyes, I saw that half of our group, twenty comrades, were preparing to leave. Comrade Rosa, in her long, gray prisoner's robe, carrying her pack, stood at the doorway about to leave. I leapt up suddenly to join her, but the guards shoved me back. A terrible thought occurred to me—we were being separated!

There was nothing either of us could do.

Quietly, Comrade Rosa threw a last, mild glance at me and quickly, in her melodic voice that pierced the clammy quiet, said words that rang in my ears for a very long time: *"Proshtshay, tovarish!"* (Farewell, comrade!)

Chapter 11

First Love

"Okay, so who's Stalin?" asked Samuel, confused by the fact that the whole family seemed to be in a tizzy. Juliette, back from Amherst for spring break and eager to share her obsessive research, gave her ten-year-old brother a quick lesson in Russian history.

"Stalin was exiled to Siberia six times in all and escaped every time—which is why, after he seized power, he created 'Gulag' forced labor camps in Siberia to contain his political enemies. These were walled and heavily guarded. No one escaped from them."

"Did Great-Grandpa Joe escape, like Stalin?" Samuel was intensely curious.

"I don't know," smiled Juliette. "You'll have to read the next chapter—like the rest of us."

Samuel was the only family member who had resisted pouncing on each installment of the translation the moment it came in from Hershl Rabinowitz, the scholar-in-residence that Juliette had found at the *Yiddish Book Center*. Unlike others in the household, who were all voracious readers, Samuel was more of an Xbox guy. Part of him wished he could "play" the Siberian Exile narrative on his console, especially the *escape* part. He was desperately curious, like everyone, about where the story was going.

Though it was maddening at first for Juliette and others to be hampered by Hershl's deliberate pace in the translation—just one chapter a month—she was now enjoying the constraint. It had created a rhythm for the year—one that was uniting the family. A crescendo of anticipation, followed by passionate debate and deconstruction. Rose, for her part, was fascinated by the fact that Joseph Rakow seemed to have met her namesake great-grandmother while in exile in Siberia.

"I'm not sure it's the same Rose," cautioned John.

"What are you talking about?" exclaimed his eldest daughter.

"This one is Rosa, not Rose," he said. "And *Mendelsohn* was not her maiden name."

"Let's call Grandma," proposed Juliette eagerly. And then everyone at the table turned to Lani with beseeching expressions—hopeful for a temporary stay of the no-device rule.

"Please, Mom," implored Rose.

Lani nodded, then glanced at John, who winked gratefully. She rolled her eyes as her device-obsessed husband speed-dialed his mother, Saralie.

"Mom," blurted John. "Is this Rosa from Siberia the same Rose that Joseph ended up marrying? Is she Grandma Rose?"

There was a pause. John had Saralie on speaker; everyone leaned in. *Why is she taking so long?*

You could tell that Saralie was enjoying herself when, finally, she responded: "You'll have to wait and see."

Twelve-year-old Joseph was particularly invested in this budding romance between his namesake ancestor and the mysterious and beautiful revolutionary girl. It reminded him of his all-consuming crush on Eva Golden, which was deepening by the minute. He could hardly sleep.

Today was the big day: their first meeting with Rabbi Weiss to discuss the *Parsha* that he and Eva would be sharing on November 3. She, no doubt, would have lots of ideas and opinions. It made Joseph nervous. He wanted to impress her. But what would he say? His great-grandfather had composed mental poetry to his beloved. Little Joseph felt so inadequate.

"Hurry up," he barked at his mother who was driving him to the synagogue. "We're going to be late!"

"We're twenty minutes early," responded Lani, eyeing her anxious son. He glared at her. "*What??*"

"You okay?" "Totally!"

He grabbed his backpack and leapt out of the car the moment they pulled to the curb— without so much as a "good-bye," let alone a "thank you."

Hormones, sighed Lani, as she drove off.

Inside the synagogue, Joseph took the steps two at a time and was out of breath as he entered the second-floor meeting room, where Eva was playing Beethoven's *Für Elise* on the upright piano in the corner—so absorbed in the music that she didn't notice him watching her from the threshold of the door. Joseph was mesmerized by her command of the composition. Was there anything Eva Golden couldn't do?

She built up soulfully to the final section of the piece, where Ludwig decided upon an insanely fast flourish of fifty-one descending sixteenth notes, played in triplets with three fingers, which Eva decided playfully to attempt with eyes closed. She went badly off the rails and then laughed at herself. That's when she noticed Joseph.

"Oh, hi," she grinned. "I messed up!"

Impossible, thought Joseph.

"You think Beethoven had a crush on Elise?" she asked.

"Who?"

"Für Elise," said Eva. "It's the name of the piece. I think it's so romantic."

If only I could compose a sonata...

"Shalom, shalom," came a voice behind them. Rabbi Weiss, a cheerful fellow in his sixties with a great passion for the Torah and its many mysteries, gestured for the kids to sit together on the settee and took his place at the armchair facing them. Joseph felt his heart skip a beat when Eva's thigh brushed against his momentarily as she sat next to him. They were awfully close! Wow…

"So, my young scholars," began the rabbi, whose trimmed beard was flecked with gray. "What do we think about *Toldot*?"

Eva jumped right in: "I love it. I can totally relate to the rivalry between Jacob and Esau.

'It's like me and my older sister. I mean I love her, of course—but I hate the way everything seems to come so easily for her. She's like the best at everything she does. It drives me crazy."

Joseph stared at Eva. It astonished him that she could actually feel "less than."

"And *you*, young man?" Rabbi Weiss turned his wise eyes to Joseph, who found himself freezing in the spotlight, momentarily tongue-tied.

The rabbi offered some additional thoughts to spark the conversation. "*Toldot* translates to 'offspring' and also 'generations,' in its multiple meanings—both, the things that we generate in our lives, our deeds and accomplishments, and also the children we will have."

He allowed space for Joseph to take this in and then asked: "Is there something you're burning to achieve?"

If only, thought the almost-teenager. *If only*…

"Jacob was the underdog, the eternal number two," said the rabbi. "Don't we all feel that way sometimes?"

That particular prompt sparked an idea in Joseph. "My dad loves underdogs," he said suddenly. "He's always working for longshot political candidates!"

"That's wonderful," said Rabbi Weiss. Then, after a pause, he added: "See if you can find a connection that's personal to *you*."

Joseph glanced nervously at Eva Golden. *If only*…

Rose Simon was painting in the sunny loft she had rented in Highland

Park, just off of York Boulevard. It was an expansive space, full of light—though the windows were south-facing, which was something of a no-no for art creation, which favors indirect lighting, rather than the contrasting brightness and shadows produced by shafts of sunlight. But the price was right—and Rose loved her studio, whose walls were stacked with canvases of varying sizes. In the front were the most recent works, which included a series of paintings she had done of her Iranian boyfriend, Bijan, on the beach. But she had since moved into a brand-new series—broody abstracts with a single recognizable motif: the proletarian hammer and sickle. She'd been inspired to move in this direction after hearing Juliette's research on societal inequality that continued to this day in both America and Russia. Rose was depicting that strife in moody, angry clouds of pigment that occupied the majority of the canvases, with the faintest hint of the communist symbol emerging like a specter through the murk. She'd been posting these new paintings online and getting a lot of support from her friends for this bold new direction.

Rose pulled out one of the four-inch wall brushes she'd bought at Home Depot and overloaded it with pigment from the can of burnt umber she'd had them custom-mix for her. Standing at a distance from her six-foot canvas, Rose imagined her great-grandfather fleeing the hailstorm of bullets in the Pinsk shtetl. Then she flicked the dripping paint at her creation with angry whips of her wrist, splattering it, Jackson Pollock-style, with blobs of "mud" and "blood." Next, Rose placed the canvas on the floor and stomped on it vigorously, running in place with her bare feet—to recreate the desperate energy of "escape." She soon found herself out of breath and only then noticed Bijan, smiling at her from the doorway to her studio, with an extravagant bouquet of three dozen red roses.

"How long have you been here?" She mock-glared to conceal her blush.

"Ten minutes." He smiled.

He'd been quietly savoring the experience of observing his beloved Rose in her artistic process, just like Joseph had been mesmerized by

Eva Golden playing the piano. Rose's passion and sensitivity were so impressive to Bijan—and had just sparked a surprising epiphany in his consciousness.

"Do you know what day this is?" he asked Rose, handing her the splendid flowers that bore her name. She was at a loss, overwhelmed momentarily by the aroma wafting up into her nostrils from a thousand ruby petals. "Our anniversary," Bijan grinned.

Rose lit up, then looked down in embarrassment. How could she have forgotten? It was exactly one year ago today that Rose and Bijan had met at the Olvera Street Market.

"So beautiful," she said, cradling the bouquet close to her heart. "So thoughtful," she gazed into his eyes with gratitude. Bijan was just getting started.

"What I'm about to say may sound a little crazy," he muttered nervously. "Bear with me. Have you read *Love in the Time of Cholera*?" he asked.

"Of course," responded Rose. García Márquez was one of her favorite writers.

"I know we're young, Rose," he continued, "but I think we've found each other." He fumbled for something in his pocket. "I don't want to wait."

As Bijan dropped to one knee, producing a diamond solitaire, Rose's jaw nearly dropped to the floor. Then, he took a deep breath and asked: "Will you marry me?"

CHAPTER 12

SORROW

The locomotive traveled angrily, spewing black clouds into the bleak, white sky. Twenty-two days had already passed since I'd been led into this infernal convoy. As much as I missed my family, with whom I'd spent every one of my fifteen years, my longing for Comrade Rosa, who I'd known less than two weeks, felt even greater. A sad loneliness pressed on my heart. Everything felt boring. This journey had no end.

With these hopeless and confused thoughts plaguing my unstimulated mind, our convoy arrived at the Ural range. As the train began approaching the mighty mountains, comrades in all of the cars crowded at the small windows, admiring the natural wonders. Finally, we had something to look at besides the lifeless steppes.

Slowly, the train began swimming on the line between two gigantic peaks. For a few seconds, it grew dark as the massive mountain obscured the sun. Prisoners pressed their curious faces against the little windows. The train moved sluggishly, its wheels screeching. And then it suddenly turned bright as a range of wondrous mountains appeared before our eyes. It occurred to me in that moment—we were no longer in Europe.

This was Asia.

After traveling over sandy deserts for four days and nights, our convoy began to reach the fields of Chelyabinsk. Here and there the earth was dotted with small trees. Herds of sheep grazed in the open fields. I saw a herdsman sitting beneath a green hillock, playing on his wooden dudka (flute). A peasant, his head bowed, followed a plow pulled by two humped camels.

The sight of farmers working the fruitful earth lifted my morose spirits and helped me endure the five more days it took us to reach the Krasnoyarsk transfer point, where Caucasian types, with their black moustaches and burning eyes, were all about, along with Letts from the Baltic region and seven-foot human giants from Mongolia. The courtyard of the lockup was noisy. More than seven hundred politicals, the majority with life sentences in Siberia, were housed in three separate buildings that stood in the center of the large yard, surrounded by a solid fence. Comrades from Finland, Estonia, South Russia, Petersburg, Moscow, Kiev, Odessa, and other industrialized parts of the Great Russian State, including the Warsaw region and nearby Polish industrial centers, were all well represented at the Krasnoyarsk transfer point. It was here that we'd be dispatched to our final destinations. Krasnoyarsk was also the site of the only major hospital in the area, so prisoners in need of medical attention were taken for treatment first, before being sent to the villages where they'd be serving out their exile. It took a few days for authorities to complete my paperwork; then I was sent, along with several comrades, on the last leg of my journey—which took place on foot, riding a bullock cart and finally by boat along the Angara River.

The wooden boat on which I and five other political exiles sat rocked terribly. Hundreds of water drops spraying from the waves beat upon our faces. Two young Kaldean women sat on the boat, skillfully maneuvering their oars. An aged peasant worked the rudder, steering the boat through the hazardous waters with the greatest caution. The boat turned and swam artfully through the dangerous underwater boulders, surmounted by rushing water. Sitting in the little boat, it seemed to me that a mighty, roaring wave would soon engulf us all and crush us into buckwheat groats.

When I asked the Kaldean girls how they dared to travel over such a dangerous river on such a flimsy wooden boat, they answered laughingly that this was not their first time on the river. "We were born here and are used to the water," said one of them.

"You will also get used to it," said the other. They were sisters, I suspected.

On July 29, 1903, I reached my assigned village of Klimeno in the Veniseysk State of Siberia. As I climbed from the rickety boat and took my first wobbly steps on the bank of the Angara River, I spotted the quaint hamlet on a tall, sandy hill—several dozen small wooden houses with long fishnets hung outside. On the shore was a small herd of cattle, waving their tails to ward off biting flies. On the lowlands, horses grazed and a large stall housed the sheep population. I heard the barking of the village dogs who galloped up to sniff us, with heavy oak chunks hanging from their necks. The peasants hung the wooden yokes on the dogs' necks to prevent them from racing around to kill the few chickens in the village. I heard barking and yowling of chained dogs everywhere. The village seemed lively, but I did not see any people. The young population, women as well as men, was in the fields, cutting and binding the green grass. Some elders met us and, approaching with great caution, delivered a peasant greeting: "How-are-you, children?" It was the first time they'd be hosting exiles.

"Akh, such young children are being sent to us! Our region must be the last and worst in the world! At your home you probably lacked for nothing, and here you will have to suffer a bit. Times change," the old peasant continued. "We natives also have troubles; when the endless winter begins, there are some foodstuffs that we can't get for any amount of money, but we are used to it. We do not know of any better life."

I looked around at the place that would be my home for the next ten years and felt a wave of emotion sweep over me. On the one hand, it was a perfectly pleasant place— even beautiful. Yet, though we'd be allowed to roam freely, this was not home. It would never be my home. My home was half-a-world away. And—given that it had taken us six weeks to get here (with escorts who knew the way and had boats, trains, and wagons)—my chance of attempting to return home on my own, before my official release, was infinitesimally small. That's why the authorities used Siberia for political exiles. It was a prison without walls.

The sheriff of Klimeno, Yakov Brukhanov, a burly, powerful man with a beard he never groomed, invited me into his home along with my political colleague Itzaak Shimanski, who was from Poland. When we entered the sheriff's house, we immediately bought a potful of sour milk mixed with cheese for ten kopeks (from the modest stipend we'd been given by the authorities to cover our living expenses). When we finished that four-square meal, I asked the sheriff about our accommodations. The stocky Asian demurred, scratching the nape of his neck.

"I don't know where I can find you lodging right now," he replied.

After a short consultation with his closest neighbor, he called several village peasants into his house.

"They don't have any money," the peasants complained. "They're just out of jail, we can't afford to house them!"

The sheriff interrupted their naive talk in a commanding voice and called out: "Listen here, dear gentlemen! These are not criminals. They are politicals and our government gives them a stipend of eight rubles a month, from which they pay their rent." The sheriff shouted at an old peasant named Batu Korshenko, who had lost all his teeth except for one. "You'll get six rubles a month for each, Batu; twelve for both."

The peasant scratched at the back of his head. A calf-like, toothless smile appeared on his gnarled face.

"But what will they eat?" he continued arguing. "I have no meat; I have preserved fish with its foul odor, but I don't know if they will eat it."

"Do you have bread and potatoes?" the sheriff replied. "That's fine. They will eat whatever you provide. They'll get used to our food. You'll give them whatever you have, and if they are not satisfied, they can look for another lodging."

With those last words the sheriff concluded his speech and Batu led us to his humble home. Upon crossing the threshold, I greeted Batu's family. All present replied politely with the expression *milosti prosim!* (Welcome, visitors.) Batu's wife, who had borne nineteen children of whom twelve survived, was sitting at that moment near a clay oven, spinning thread from flax. Several young Kaldean girls sat on long wooden benches, weaving a net. These minor-age children of the house, seeing two unfamiliar persons, became frightened and stopped their spinning.

On orders from old Batu, the housewife immediately heated up the samovar and offered us a few glasses of brick tea. Then the old man pointed us to an empty storage room. The walls were smoke-stained and covered with dust. Heaps of flax were scattered across the floor. A few pairs of leather boots, smeared in tar, lay in a corner. Two tin-covered chests, painted in several colors, stood in the middle of the space. Carrying in an old wooden table with two chairs and an old worn-out deerskin, the peasant said to us: "Now you have a fine dwelling. Here on the ground, on this soft deerskin, you will be able to sleep."

When I examined the pelt, from which clumps of hair kept falling, I burst out laughing. The man in his long beard and shaggy, unshorn hair was perplexed by our unexpected laughter.

"If my room doesn't please you, you're free to go!" the peasant said, angrily.

"No," I replied. "I am satisfied with the room. But please tell me, sir landlord, how old is this deerskin?"

Putting part of his beard into his mouth and scratching the nape of his neck, the man replied: "It must be about fifteen years since I shot that deer in the woods."

"How long can the skin still be used?" I asked.

Batu laughed good-naturedly and replied: "The skin is good to be used for another twenty-five years; falling hair is no matter. The more the hair falls, the better the deerskin looks."

With this, he left us to rest. As soon as the Polish exile and I stretched out on the deerskin, we were immediately attacked by a gang of parasites. All night I fought a battle with the biting bedbugs and flying mosquitoes. By the time dawn arrived, my eyes were bugging out. I had been unable to sleep a wink. When Batu arose, I confronted him and asked what was to be done about the bedbugs.

"I will drive them off at once!" he replied. "They don't bite us. You'll get used to it," he consoled us. Bringing in a bottle of kerosene, Batu poured it all around our sleeping area. But the fumes were so noxious, it almost made matters worse. I told my roommate Itzaak that I intended to find different lodgings and went about house to house, seeing if someone would take me in. But, one after another, they found an excuse to turn me away. Just as I was about to resign myself to return to the bedbugs and kerosene fumes, a woman summoned me from behind a tree. She had kind, gypsy-like eyes. She told me she lived on her own in the woods just outside of town and that I was welcome to stay in her home. The front door of her cottage was adorned with a feathered dreamcatcher, and I sensed that she was some kind of medicine woman. The house was very spartan, but far cleaner than the sty belonging to Batu. When she told me her name was Sarnai (which meant "Rose" in Mongolian), I knew that I was in the right place.

Having made my choice of lodging, it did not take me long to assimilate. Bit by bit, I began to accede to the demands of Asiatic life in the lonely Kaldean village.

Chapter 13

Pride

"That bitch looks like a witch," said Jake Trent, youngest son of the incumbent congressman from Texas, who was part of the campaign. "How about we have some fun with her?"

He was showing his dad a picture that Alexa Alvarado had posted a few years back on Instagram of her mom on a farm, messing around with a live chicken. A laughing Patti was holding the flustered bird by its wings and making a crazy face, mugging for the camera. Jake, who'd just graduated from Texas A&M with a degree in marketing, was proposing the idea of altering the image to make Trent's Democrat challenger appear ghoulish and leaking it to the press. His father was proud of Jake. He was learning how to play the game. All was fair in love and war. And politics.

Rose Simon still couldn't get over what had just happened between her and Bijan. They were barely in their twenties, but Bijan seemed so much wiser and more mature—maybe it had to do with being from a different culture, one which went back millennia. Rose felt younger somehow—and, like her newer country, she was still trying to work certain things out. She thought of that song from *The Sound of Music*, which she and her sister had watched a million times as kids, where Rolf sings to Liesl about being unprepared to a face a world of men.

What was so great about her relationship with Bijan was that Rose felt she could share anything with him, including her neurosis about being totally unprepared to face the *world of men*. It turns out that *The Sound of Music* had been a family favorite in the Yadzani household, too—and Bijan, knowing most of the lyrics by heart, sang the continuation of Rolf's verse to Rose as they drove up the coast for one of their weekend picnics.

They laughed and then went strolling down the beach, hand in hand.

After his astonishing full-court press, Bijan had backed off completely to give Rose all the time she needed. A "proposal" is exactly what it means, he had said. Something to consider. And he wanted her to take all the time she needed to respond. Years, if necessary.

"I'm not going anywhere," he smiled.

Rose couldn't believe this guy. It was girls, she thought, who were usually supposed to figure this stuff out first, right? Initially, Bijan had wanted to get the blessing of her father before he proposed, but he'd had second thoughts about it—and Rose was sure glad he'd hesitated.

"Dad would've been even more freaked out than me," she confided. They decided to keep it secret for the time being, lest external forces intercede to influence their thinking. Bijan knew it was uncommon to marry so early in the West. His reasoning was that he wanted to be young enough to enjoy his grandkids, maybe even great-grandkids.

Whoa, thought Rose.

"I know, I know," he grinned. He was miles ahead of her.

Patti's husband, Enrique Alvarado, was a happy man as he drove his pickup truck to the construction site where he was framing a house in the upscale Flour Bluff neighborhood of Corpus Christi. He was feeling gratitude and joy at being married to such an extraordinary woman. This was a big day for them—an anniversary. Not of their wedding, seven years ago, but of the day they first met, which was seven years prior to that. Seven and seven. Two lucky numbers.

Enrique felt fortunate, certainly, to be wed to a woman who fourteen years earlier had snuck across the border illegally with her infant daughter and was now running for Congress. What a powerful example for refugees. Enrique had met Patti through his sister, Maria, who worked as a social worker, helping migrants navigate the system. Maria had felt so much compassion for Patti that she offered her a room at the family compound that Enrique had built just outside of Corpus Christi for the Alvarado clan. That's when Enrique and Patti had fallen in love.

Given the trauma she'd been through with her first husband, Enrique gave her plenty of time to warm up to the idea of another marriage. It took seven years. But it felt to Enrique like the blink of an eye. That newborn girl whom Patti had carried across the border, and whom Enrique had later adopted, had just celebrated her *quinceañera*, now on her way to becoming an impressive woman like her mother. Enrique could not have been prouder of both of them.

But, as he drove to work that morning in the summer of 2018, something caught his eye that made Enrique slam on his brakes. He stared at a campaign placard on a lawn, created and distributed, clearly, by the Trent campaign. It was an image of his wife with a chicken, but they had manipulated it grotesquely in Photoshop, so she now had fangs, bloodshot eyes, and even a set of pointy horns growing from her skull. The chicken had been splattered with blood, as if part of a pagan ritual. What made Enrique truly enraged was the printed text: "Voodoo Mexican Witch Believes in Animal Sacrifice!" Then in big block letters: *NOT IN AMERICA.*

With a surge of adrenaline, Enrique leapt from his vehicle and stomped across the lawn. He yanked the sign from the earth in disgust and snapped its wooden stake over his knee. He was already seething as he tossed the broken placard in the back of his truck and pulled away;

then he came upon a second sign, and a third. They were dotted up and down the residential street. Enrique felt his blood beginning to boil as he lurched down the block, yanking up and destroying every sign he came across. One homeowner was outside collecting mail as Enrique charged across his lawn.

"Hey!" yelled the man. "What the heck??"

Enrique didn't bother answering. He was on a mission, sprinting to the next lawn, where another placard was affronting his wife. Then he noticed a Cadillac parked across the street with its trunk popping open. Jake Trent hopped out and grabbed a sign and his hammer from the trunk, then walked up to the porch to ring the doorbell. A housewife responded and Jake turned on the charm. Enrique couldn't hear the content of their conversation, but there was plenty of laughter—especially after Jake showed the woman his inflammatory sign.

"Sure, go right ahead," she seemed to indicate. Jake tipped his cowboy hat and went to find the most favorable position on her lawn with the highest visibility. As he began hammering the stake into the ground, Enrique charged across the street, yelling: "*Hijo de puta!!*"

He shoved Jake backward. Even though the beefy frat boy had sixty pounds on him, Enrique was a scrappy street fighter and went after Jake with a vengeance. "How dare you?" he yelled. "No one insults my wife!!"

They rolled on the ground for a few moments, fists flying. Neighbors emerged from their homes to watch the unfolding brawl. Enrique swung left and right, heart pounding with rage and indignation. Jake managed to slip away and then did something that changed everything—he pulled a gun. It had been hidden in a holster under his jacket. Jake aimed the Colt .45 squarely at his Hispanic assailant. "Fight's over, motherfucker," snarled Jake. "You're under arrest."

"You loco?" Enrique snarled right back at him. "You're no cop."

"I'm a United States citizen," snapped Jake. "But I guess you wouldn't know what that means."

"I'm a citizen, too," Enrique retorted.

"Then you must know about our right to make a citizen's arrest." Jake aimed the gun squarely at Enrique's head.

"On what grounds?" demanded Enrique, who was growing increasingly agitated.

"Let me think," mused Jake, counting them out on his free hand. "How about—assault, trespassing, vandalism, destruction of private property... And you might want to know that we also have something called a 'Constitution' here in America," Jake continued condescendingly, "whose First Amendment protects my right to post signs like this one." He picked up the fallen placard and hammered it into the lawn. "It's called 'Free Speech.'"

Enrique backed off, clearly defeated: "Okay, you've made your point."

"Don't move, asshole." Jake narrowed his eyes, pulling out his phone and dialing 9-1-1. "You're going to jail."

By evening, Enrique's mugshot was everywhere. All three networks were carrying the story, which seemed to contain every hot-button issue of the day: immigration, the First and Second Amendments, Free Speech versus Fake News. It was irresistible.

Patti called John on the way to the Nueces County Jail, having decided to bail her husband out in person, which he thought was a disastrous idea—like gasoline on a fire. The press corps, already in a frenzy, would certainly pounce. "No comments whatsoever," he cautioned. "Let me figure this out."

In the absence of sound bites from the Alvarados, the media went over to the other camp, where Ralph Trent was all too happy to go on the record. "The United States of America is a nation of law and order," he told reporters, "not some banana republic where we condone vigilante justice."

Good one, thought John, in grudging admiration—wondering, again, who was coaching the congressman.

"No response is killing you," said Juliette, who'd been following the story from her Amherst dorm room. But John trusted his gut in crisis situations, and his instinct was telling him to sit this one out. There was no way to spin it in their favor without walking into a minefield. As heinous as he'd been in creating that offensive caricature, Jake Trent hadn't broken the law like Enrique.

Juliette hung up, dissatisfied, and headed to the library, determined to use her newfound investigative skills to find an angle. And boy did she succeed.

One hour later, she called her father back in excitement to explain that she had reason to believe that Jake Trent may have also broken the law. Juliette had a strong hunch that Jake didn't have a license to carry his concealed weapon, that he hadn't registered the gun with the Texas Department of Public Safety.

"How in the world could you know that?" John asked his daughter in astonishment.

Juliette had discovered a letter that Jake Trent had written to the editor of *The Battalion*—the student paper at Texas A&M, where he'd gone to school—in which he espoused extreme libertarian views that there should be no restrictions whatsoever to gun ownership. He thought Americans should have the right to conceal and carry without any form of government control.

John was amazed. If true, this could be exactly what they needed to turn the tables. He called a contact at the FBI, who confirmed Juliette's hunch to be correct, which meant Jake Trent's citizen arrest of Enrique Alvarado had been illegal. They were forced to drop the charges and release him.

"I'm proud of my wife," Enrique told reporters outside the jail. "Woe to the man who disrespects her!"

That's when Patti's poll numbers began to rise.

CHAPTER 14

SURVIVAL

Once the snow began to fall in Siberia, it never stopped.

I had arrived in the balm of summer, with its gentle breezes and buzzing flies. Just a few months later, the terrain had become a wasteland. Dead silence ruled the village. Frosty winds swept across the frigid mountains. And everyone stayed indoors to avoid the bitter cold.

I began to write in a journal that I purchased with my stipend from a trader who passed through the remote Siberian villages with a wagon of provisions and sundry supplies. I wrote about everything that had transpired since my arrest in Pinsk. In hopes of an eventual reunion with my family, I wanted to make sure I remembered all the details. I also recorded my dreams, which, for reasons unknown to me, had become more vivid since arriving in Siberia. I composed poetry; I wrote about Comrade Rosa. I even journaled about my hunger—food had become scarce.

One day, I went ice-fishing with some of Batu's children, who laughed at my difficulty in negotiating the thick snowdrifts and branches that snapped rudely into my face as I fought my way through the barren forest—while they frolicked along without a care, leading us to the frozen river basin.

I watched Arban, one of Batu's six sons, who was a few years older than me, as he sawed a small hole in the ice where he dropped his fishing line. Within a few minutes, he had caught his first fish—a foot-long perch that, in its desperation to survive, had snapped at Arban's lure, fashioned from animal hair to resemble a fly.

It seemed simple enough, so I decided to give it a go. I had made my own lure and borrowed an ice saw. I went looking for an appropriate place to cut my hole. But my inexperience at reading the ice proved to be my downfall. I heard a sudden crack.

Everyone turned in alarm as the ice sheet disintegrated beneath me. I had chosen an area that was too thin and plunged suddenly into the glacial water. It was so cold, I felt my body had been impaled by daggers. I gasped, struggling for air.

Arban and his siblings rushed to find a branch they could extend in my direction, knowing how quickly I could succumb to frostbite or even death if hypothermia set in.

The first branch they found wasn't long enough. The frost, by now, had penetrated every part of my body. My feet began to freeze. Arban came back with a second branch, which was able, thankfully, to reach me. I flailed desperately to grab ahold of it, hanging on for dear life as they dragged me out of the water. Now, we had to get me indoors and near a hearth as quickly as possible.

They told me to take off my clothes, which seemed counterintuitive at first. But as I felt the soaked material freezing stiff around my limbs, I realized it would severely limit my ability to move. My teeth began to chatter as I removed my iced clothing, then they helped me trudge back to the village through snowy woods. I cut myself, clambering over fallen branches; but I didn't feel anything because my limbs felt paralyzed. At a certain point, I must have blacked out.

Next thing I knew, I was back in Sarnai's hut, bundled up in furs and warming up near the iron stove. She was treating my skin with an herbal salve and had brewed a special medicinal tea for me to drink, but I had trouble swallowing anything. My tonsils had ballooned up with infection, and my throat was severely constricted. She tried to give me ice chips to keep me hydrated, but I had no energy to suck on them.

My symptoms were quickly escalating. I threw off the covers, having spiked a fever that made it feel as though there were lava flowing through my veins. My lungs became thick with mucus. The sheriff appeared, along with other villagers who were now gravely concerned about my health. Sarnai tried to shoo them away, explaining that she had the situation under control—but Sheriff Brukhanov would not accept her assessment. Apparently, there was some tension between them. This was the first time the village of Klimeno had been assigned political refugees, and the sheriff was concerned that there could be consequences if I died on their watch. The sheriff was skeptical of Sarnai's plant medicine and made the executive decision that I was to be taken by horse to the hospital in Krasnoyarsk. Thus, I was loaded with blankets onto a long-haired Yakutian horse, roped to a second horse ridden by Arban—and off we went. My recollection of our journey to Krasnoyarsk was blurred by fever and exhaustion. But I managed somehow, chilled, sick, and broken, to reach the hospital.

The chief surgeon, Dr. Nikolai Orlov, and several of his colleagues examined me with great consternation. My tonsils were so swollen at this point that they impeded my ability to ingest food, and even to breathe. Tonsillitis could be a very serious condition, Dr. Orlov explained. He told me that the first US president, George Washington, had actually died of the condition. There was a procedure, relative safe, going back to Roman times and increasingly popular, to remove the infected tonsils. French doctors had recently invented a device—the tonsil "guillotine"—to simplify the operation, which he urgently recommended. The doctor was being kind in explaining all of this to me in such detail. As a prisoner, he did not need my consent to treat me. But I was a minor, and he could tell I was scared.

I looked at Dr. Orlov in gratitude—thankful to be in the hands of such a caring professional. They administered ether by placing a glass globe over my mouth, and I quickly lost consciousness.

Next thing I remember was waking up in the postsurgical recovery ward where shafts of sunlight streamed through tall windows. My tonsils were gone and I felt much better. There were nearly sixty people in the long, second-story hallway, lying in cots along the walls. Nurses went from bed to bed, checking on sutures and bandages. A pair of guards with bayonets stood on either end of the hallway, keeping an eye on the political prisoners, who were being kept in a designated area to distinguish them from ordinary, civilian patients. I looked around at my revolutionary comrades with pride and affection. Some were young like me, others older, both male and female, from every corner of Russia—all united in the single cause of justice for workers everywhere. As I scanned the courageous faces, I saw a young woman smiling at me from across the hall.

"Yosef," she whispered.

I couldn't believe my eyes.

It was Minne—my sister's friend from Pinsk (who'd worked with her at the match factory)! By an extraordinary act of kismet, we'd both been exiled and injured at the same time. She snuck over to my bed, and we shared the details of our arrests and detention. She was serving ten years like me in the town of Targiz near the Angara River, where, in an escape attempt, she had fractured her arm, which was now bandaged in a splint. Minne glanced around quickly to check on the guards, then leaned in close to whisper words that made my heart leap.

"I have news of your family," she said, explaining that through the revolutionary grapevine, she'd heard that my parents and siblings had made it safely to Hamburg, where they'd boarded a boat to the "New World." They were going to America!

My eyes widened. I was desperate for more details, but guards intervened to pull us apart. That night, I hardly slept a wink. Waiting until midnight, when the night shift sentry, Dmitriy Popovi, fell asleep—it happened like clockwork every evening after the watchman secretly sipped vodka from a flask he kept in his coat pocket—I took out my mother's pearl earring, which I'd hidden so many times in my mouth (and sometimes even swallowed to protect). I imagined Sonya gazing at the earring's twin on the other side of the world. My mind played out fantasies of reunion with my family in America. I pictured the "skyscrapers" that Max had talked about, buildings so tall, they literally scratched at the heavens—the "Mighty Palaces" of my youthful imagination. I began hatching plans for an escape.

The following day, I managed to sneak in a brief moment with Minne in which she shared valuable information. She, too, had been pondering the idea of an escape, which was possible, she thought, even during the cold months of winter—it actually provided an advantage, as the rivers were frozen over, which meant they could be navigated with horses and sleds. Devoid of trees and Cossack patrols, they also provided geographic certainty—you couldn't get lost following a river. In Krasnoyarsk, we were on Yenisei, one of the largest rivers in Asia. The mighty waterway, which we could see from the windows of our recovery room, appeared entirely frozen over. Normally, it flowed northwest a thousand miles to the Barents Sea, above Scandinavia.

"That's our roadway to freedom," whispered Minne.

She was so convinced of her plan that I didn't dare mention my own disastrous experience plummeting through the ice on a supposedly frozen river. The temperatures had fallen significantly since then, making the surface ice more reliable, perhaps. The idea began to percolate in my mind. Through the window near my bed, I spotted an old sled in the hospital yard below. Was this dream attainable?

Minne certainly thought so. We began secretly hoarding potatoes and other supplies. There would be a full moon, one week from now—this would be our best opportunity to sneak out under darkness. The guard Dmitriy would reliably fall asleep at some point, but the sentries manning the hospital's main entrance were always vigilant. Therefore, we planned to fashion a makeshift rope from torn-up bedsheets to descend out back through the second-story windows.

That night, after Dmitriy began to snore, my mission was to sneak down the to the supply closet at the end of the hall to get bedsheets for our rope, while Minne stood as a lookout. The corridor was littered with patients sleeping in cots and on the floor, since the hospital was overcrowded. I weaved through the slumbering bodies and came to the storage closet—not surprised to discover that a cot had also been crammed into this small room, too. But what was flabbergasting was the person who happened to be sleeping in this particular bed: it was Comrade Rosa!

I stared at her in speechless shock. Though her face was pale, she was sleeping peacefully. I gazed at her beauty, remembering the time we slept next to each other in the filthy, crowded cell in Samara. I must have lost track of time as I savored the moment, for, next thing I knew, Minne rushed up, almost giving me a heart attack.

"What's taking you so long?" she hissed.

I turned, at a loss. "I know her."

Minne could tell from my expression that I had feelings for Comrade Rosa. But we had to get back to our ward before the alarm was raised. Minne grabbed my hand, a stack of sheets, and led us back to the recovery room, where, for the rest of that night, we each worked diligently underneath our covers to rip the sheets, as quietly as we could, into strips we'd weave together to create a rope that would be strong enough to support our weight. My mind was swimming with thoughts. What about Comrade Rosa? Could we bring her? Was she healthy enough to escape?

The following day brought a surprise that changed everything. Minne was abruptly escorted out of the dormitory by a Cossack guard, who would be escorting her back to her village. My heart sank. Minne turned around to face me just before leaving. She raised her fist in the revolutionary salute and placed it over her heart in solidarity. I did the same. Then the guard shoved her into the hall. I was saddened by the feeling that this was the last time I'd ever see her.

That night, though I no longer had Minne as my lookout, I darted urgently down the hall to reconnect with Comrade Rosa. Upon entering the storage room to find her, again, sleeping like an angel, I couldn't help but just watch for a moment.

Then, quite spontaneously, as if sensing my presence, she opened her eyes. I surged with elation, grinning foolishly. Comrade Rosa gazed back at me with an expression of tenderness.

"Comrade Yosef," she smiled sweetly. "How did I know I would see you again?"

We rapidly shared stories. I learned that she was an orphan, having lost her entire family to the Cossack assassins. After settling into her village of Ilansky, she was taken to Krasnoyarsk with a life-threatening case of pneumonia, which she'd contracted after losing her way in a blizzard. She was now, thankfully, fully healed, like myself—and we were being held in the hospital simply because the local authorities lacked the manpower at the moment to escort us individually to our respective villages.

Knowing that our time together was precious, I grabbed some blankets and convinced her to sneak onto the roof, where stars, in their infinite glory, filled the sky.

Mustering my courage, I recited the poem I had written for beautiful Comrade Rosa:

For Rosa—

Last night I closed my eyes with thoughts of you
Floating through my mind like a sweet melody,
And dreamed I touched my finger to your cheek—
Your beauty flushed like the skin of a rose,
Your gaze so clear and brave and bright, glowing
Like two stars in the bitter cold of the night.
And though the icy breath of winter bit
And tore at our clothes and the silk of your hair,
Your eyes were warm: they spoke to me in holy silence
Of distant skies, golden plains and violet peaks—
Of vast horizons where the sun dips into stormy seas
And great countries where the sun sets on the free.
I woke and knew I'd found the answer to our cries
Within the shining promise of your eyes.

Comrade Rosa was deeply touched. She raised her delicate hand and placed it against my cheek. After a moment of looking into my eyes, she leaned forward and pressed her soft lips against mine. I felt a tingling running up and down my spine. It was my first kiss.

We sat in silence for a moment, marveling at the impressive Krasnoyarsk Railway Bridge that spanned the frozen river, a feat of engineering that had won a prize, I was told, at the Paris Exposition. Reminding me of the West, I turned to Comrade Rosa and exclaimed: "Come with me to America!"

I explained the escape plan along the river that Minne and I had been planning. I thought, with her own family gone, she needed a fresh start. The West could give us that. The journey would be long and dangerous, I knew—but I was convinced that, together, we could do it. To my great joy, she agreed.

Time was of the essence. Any moment, the authorities could separate us, once again, and send us back to our respective villages. So we resolved to go the following night, though it was still shy of a full moon.

My heart was pounding in anticipation as evening grew near. I couldn't wait for the watchman to drink his vodka. It seemed to be taking forever. He was upset, it seemed, at how little remained in his flask and went to get an additional bottle from a hidden cache. When, finally, he leaned back in his chair and began breathing deeply, I grabbed the supplies I had hidden under my bunk and raced down the hallway where Comrade Rosa was all set to go. She had her hair back to look like a boy.

We darted to the window at the end of the hall and pried it open, careful not to make a sound. When I secured our makeshift rope to an iron bar near the window and threw it down, we became aware of our first challenge: the rope was not long enough. It would require an eight-foot leap to the ground—not impossible, since the fall would be cushioned by snow. But it could make noise.

I resolved to go first and test it out. With Comrade Rosa watching from above, I lowered myself, hand over fist, surprised at how cold it was. Without gloves, my hands became numb, and I worried I might lose my grip. Finally, near the end of the rope, I dropped into the snowdrift. Dusting off the flakes, I waved up to Comrade Rosa, who pulled up the rope, tied off our sack of supplies, and lowered them down. So far, so good. Now it was her turn. But Comrade Rosa turned from the window and disappeared suddenly. Where did she go? Did someone catch her? All sorts of dire scenarios played themselves out in my imagination as I waited below. It felt interminably long. Then finally she reappeared with a smile. What was that thing she was waving in her hand?

I suddenly realized—a revolver! I shuddered to imagine where she had procured that. Had she stolen it from the sleeping guard? Comrade Rosa placed the gun in her belt, then she came down the rope, much more nimbly than I had. I caught her in my arms and realized, of course, she was considerably lighter than I.

"How on earth did you get that?!" I asked about the revolver.

"I have my ways," she smiled. "Have you ever fired one?"

I responded in the affirmative, but she detected a hesitancy in my voice. "I'll hold onto it," she declared.

We surveyed the landscape ahead of us. I proposed heading for the distant tree line, where there was a row of evergreens that would provide some cover. We exchanged a smile and readied ourselves. Then suddenly we were running—or perhaps "trudging" better describes it. While in truth it was difficult to progress through the deep snow, I felt so happy and full of hope. With Comrade Rosa at my side, it seemed as if anything were possible. For the first time in months, I felt free.

But just as we reached the tree cover, we heard a whistle in the distance. Moments later, the sound of barking dogs. We glanced at each other in sudden concern. We needed a place to hide.

"The barn," said Comrade Rosa, pointing to a nearby structure. We scurried over, pulled open the door, whose frozen hinges squeaked. Inside there were horses that snorted restlessly as we entered. There was also a sled, which could come in handy.

"We had one of these back home," said Comrade Rosa, crossing to the sled. Then her eyes became wistful. I knew she was thinking about the family she had lost, and I felt badly for her.

Comrade Rosa turned to me suddenly and said: "I need you to make me a promise, Comrade Yosef." I stared at her solemnly, wondering what was coming next.

"No matter what happens, you will never look back. You will never stop trying.

You will find your family in America. Do I have your word?" "Not without you," I protested.

"I'll be at your side," she assured me. "But as long as you still have a family, do you promise you will stop at nothing to find them?"

I looked into her eyes and said: "I do."

Satisfied with my response, she led one of the horses out of its stall and harnessed it to the sled. We listened for the dogs and peered through the crack in the door. The sounds were distant. The dogs, thankfully, had not picked up our trail. But it was only a matter of time. Comrade Rosa said we should use the sled to distance ourselves from the hospital, without leaving more tracks or scents in the snow. It was a good plan.

Comrade Rosa told me to get on the sled and take its reins. She drew the revolver, slowly opened the squeaky barn doors, and cautiously peered outside. The coast seemed clear. We were shielded from view of the distant hospital by the row of evergreens we ran past to get to the barn.

Very gently, she led the horse out of the barn, clicking her tongue to calm it. I waited, reins in hand, as she went to close the barn doors. Then we heard a voice that made us jump: "Stop where you are!"

It was Dmitriy. He was alone and appeared to be slightly inebriated. But Dmitriy had his rifle drawn and meant business. He was panning it back and forth between me on the sled and Comrade Rosa, who was back at the barn doors, having just closed them. She, too, had her gun drawn.

"Drop your weapon!" she yelled at Dmitriy.

"Drop yours!" he shouted back at her, turning the rifle on me for a moment, then back to Comrade Rosa. It reminded me suddenly of the awful moment back in Pinsk, when my brother Max and I were pinned by guards on opposite sides of the courtyard, as we tried to escape.

"Drop your weapon or I'll shoot!" screamed Comrade Rosa. "I'll shoot you first!" he threatened.

Comrade Rosa turned to me, "Shake the reins! Go!"

I hesitated. "Go!!" she repeated. "You promised you would go!"

I had a terrible feeling about where this was going...

I was frozen; she was furious, and Dmitriy was becoming increasingly agitated. "I'll shoot you both!" he screamed.

"Go, Comrade," cried Rosa, practically in tears. "Before the reinforcements come!" I found myself pulled in two directions, not knowing what to do.

And that's when everything unraveled.

Dmitriy fired his rifle. Comrade Rosa fired her gun. They both went down.

I screamed, seeing that she'd received a fatal wound to her chest. She fell to the ground, turning her head in my direction. My eyes widened in horror as blood dripped from her beautiful mouth into the snow. Dmitriy had received a grave wound to his shoulder, too, which had also landed him on the ground and sent his rifle flying.

Comrade Rosa fixed me with her gaze and croaked her final word: "Go..."

But I couldn't move. Even as the barking grew louder.

All I could do was drop the reins, hold my head. And sob.

Chapter 15

The Tears Will Never Dry

It was beyond heartbreaking.

Unable to contain her swirling emotions, Juliette picked up the phone to call her dad. This was not about the latest chapter of Joseph Rakow's memoir, however. It concerned something that had just occurred in Corpus Christi.

The tragedy of Comrade Rosa's apparent death had been mirrored by a modern-day shooting—one that had dire implications for Patti Alvarado, and therefore for John Simon, too.

"You okay, Dad?" asked Juliette.

"Hanging in there," he said. "About to jump on a plane."

Earlier that morning—June 23, 2018, at 7:15 a.m.—a bright but troubled teen named Dexter Jones had boarded a city bus to go to a summer camp program in "Underwater Robotics" at the Corpus Christi campus of Texas A&M. Alexa Alvarado, Patti's fifteen-year-old daughter who had a passion for marine biology, happened to be attending the same program.

Dexter, who was gifted in math but had sensory integration issues that made it difficult for him in school—especially in social situations—had received a scholarship to attend the program. Things were especially tough at home these days for the sixteen-year-old; he had just shaved his head, following the suicide of his estranged father. A latchkey kid, Dexter lived alone with his single mom who worked two jobs to make ends meet. She blamed their economic woes on "the goddamn Mexicans."

Dexter was angry. Depressed. And didn't have an outlet.

After thinking about it for weeks, the despondent boy had snuck into his mother's room that morning, opened the dresser drawer, and lifted out her Smith & Wesson .38 snub-nosed revolver, which could fit easily into his backpack. He popped open the cylinder to make sure it contained six rounds, then grabbed an extra box of ammo for good measure. No one would have guessed, as Dexter rode alone in the back row of the bus, what he was about to do.

He started firing the moment he arrived on campus. Anyone Hispanic.

People darted for cover in all directions, screaming in pandemonium. A campus cop heard the shots and sprang into action. He approached Dexter, gun drawn, as the boy was reloading.

The cop yelled at him to drop his weapon. Dexter refused. He was shot dead on the spot.

The whole thing lasted less than four minutes.

Campus went into lockdown. Three students lay dead, one seriously injured. All Latino. What was particularly disturbing were posts that Dexter had been making on social media, calling for a racial jihad against Mexicans. His father, before committing suicide, had been a staunch supporter of Ralph Trent.

As before, Congressman Trent hit the airwaves first in a series of preemptive reiterations of standard NRA talking points—"the aftermath of a tragedy is no time to discuss curtailing gun rights," "liberals always use incendiary moments like these to propose limits on the Second Amendment." But Trent, as he was wont to do, went even further.

"Thank God for guns," he declared with unabashed fervor. "Without

the good use of a gun, this situation would've been a heckuva lot worse."
He was referring, of course, to the campus cop.

John landed at 2 p.m. local time and was huddling with the Alvarados within the hour. The thing that had shaken them more than anything was the possibility, given the support by Dexter's father of Ralph Trent, that Alexa Alvarado, specifically, could have been an intended target.

Patti had arrived at the campus in a panic. The media was every-where. Aware that PTSD from her first husband's murder in Matamoros had been retriggered, she was smart enough to avoid making any public comment, as John had implored. After the lockdown was lifted, Patti and Alexa were reunited and went for a private walk, weeping together and processing the raw emotions.

Patti told Alexa that she was withdrawing from the race. Family came first. But Alexa wouldn't have it. Strong and stubborn like her mom, Alexa told her to fight even harder.

"Even if I had died," she said with certainty, "I would've wanted you to keep going."

Patti stared. "Are you sure?"

"I've never been more positive in my life." Her brown eyes were unwavering.

Patti was so proud of the incredible girl she had the privilege to call her daughter. She took a deep breath and nodded. So be it.

By 3 p.m., she brought Alexa into the huddle with her war council—which included John and Enrique, among others.

"I want to talk to the mothers who lost their kids," declared Patti. "Good idea," nodded John. "I'll call CNN to offer them an exclusive."

"We're starting with Mrs. Jones," said Patti.

Jones…? People were confused. That name wasn't Mexican.

"The shooter's mom," explained Patti.

John nodded vigorously. Brilliant move.

"Alexa's idea," smiled Patti, pulling her daughter close.

"Thank G-d for our kids," said John with a grin. "Somebody's gotta keep us honest," agreed Enrique.

That evening, the press came out in droves as the Alvarado caravan descended upon the modest bungalow where Melba Jones was holed up, downing her third shot of bourbon. Patti was carrying a platter as she walked up to the porch. She had to ring the bell three times.

Mrs. Jones emerged, finally, in a housedress, squinting with suspicion.

"I'm very sorry for your loss," said Patti, as flashbulbs popped in a fusillade. "I lost my first husband to violence," she continued. "I know what it's like."

"You people oughta go on home," said Melba, with a special emphasis on the word *people*.

Patti held her ground. "I brought you some food, Mrs. Jones." She extended the tray, which contained homemade tamales.

"Don't particularly care for your type of cooking," responded Melba.

"Take it," insisted Patti. "These were homemade by my daughter, Alexa, who was in the camp with your son." Patti stared pointedly into the woman's eyes and pushed the tray into her hands. Melba took a deep breath, then turned without a word and closed the door.

Inside the dark kitchen, with jittery roaches scurrying across her unwashed plates, Melba emptied the homemade tamales into the trash can. Then, leaning against the counter to keep from falling—she wept.

Outside, Patti marched into the waiting car without mirth. "Who's got tequila?" she demanded.

She was shaking.

CHAPTER 16

THERE ARE NO WORDS

Many winters passed before I was able to write again. The pages that follow are fragmentary recollections, reconstructed years after these events occurred—for, when the authorities finally returned me, broken and despairing, to the dreary village of Klimeno, where I was to serve out the remainder of my time, I was numb, half-dead—with little desire to continue living. The only thing that kept me going was the solemn promise I had made to Comrade Rosa—not to give up, no matter what.

The endless Siberian winters hardly helped. The sun would disappear for months on end. And the cheerless, gray daylight came and went in a matter of hours. Bleak doesn't come close to describe the pervasive desolation. Death was everywhere.

With nothing to do, my mind became a claustrophobic cauldron of neurotic thoughts, plagued with guilt and self-judgment. I kept replaying what had happened to Comrade Rosa. What if I had answered differently when she had asked me about my knowledge of guns? I'd fired a revolver numerous times, last spring when I'd fled the country and was working on the farm in Austria—but I had answered haltingly. What if I had been more bold?

Maybe she would have given me the gun to hold instead of her, which meant she'd still be alive.

In the absence of stimulation, I tortured myself endlessly with these hypothetical scenarios of what could have been. The snow kept falling. And falling.

Would the winter never end?

Then, in an annual miracle, icicles began to drip. Geese crossed the sky in impressive chevron formations, returning to their breeding grounds in the north. Saplings began pushing through the melting snow. Squirrels scurried from the trees, furrowing for the caches of nuts they'd buried before frost blanketed everything. And suddenly the world came back to life, with nature, once again, dancing its wild quadrille.

It was impressive to me. The unrelenting, inextinguishable drive of nature to express and regenerate, again and again. Every year, the spring renewal would boost my spirits—though it came late in Siberia, closer to summer, really. And, with it arrived another set of trials, such as the infernal flies that swarmed like locusts and mosquitoes whose bites became torturous welts on every limb.

My biggest challenge, however, was boredom. The decade I spent in Siberia, between ages fifteen and twenty-five, should have been the prime of my learning and formation of my intellect. I yearned for books and stimulation. I longed for knowledge and mentors. All I had were sheep. I came to realize why the tsarist authorities sent us here. Siberia had a way of quashing the fire within us. The monotonous, ordinary daily life in exile began to disgust me.

Nonetheless, there were moments, here and there, that I shall always cherish, such as my relationship with the gentle Sarnai, who became like a second mother to me and showed me the ways of the woods. She taught me the names and functions of the native plants and folk remedies that went back generations. I also learned the Kaldean language, customs, and some of their history.

Before my second winter, I gathered a beautifully gnarled knot of oak and carved it into the shape of a rose. When the snow came, I would clasp my "rose" in both hands and hold it near my heart to help me endure the endless months of indoor isolation, which became almost unbearable, like an extended period of solitary confinement—even though I was not actually alone. Sarnai's presence did not feel like company, during the grueling months of the first few winters. Despite my growing fondness for her, when the snow came, Sarnai began to irritate me; everything about her—the way she would hum incessantly, her slightly halting gait, even the way she breathed. But what drove me to almost murderous thoughts was the way Sarnai would look at me with those "knowing" eyes of hers and shake her head sadly.

"It's in your mind," she would say, pointing at her head—"you're a prisoner in your own mind." I'd grumble and sulk and pray for spring. She'd shake her head and even laugh sometimes. I wanted to kill her.

Over the course of numerous conversations, partially pantomimed to overcome language barriers, Sarnai tried to communicate a simple fact—the only way to survive the merciless Siberian winters was to embrace them fully, to become deeply present, even curious about the darkness, biting cold, the stillness, absence of color, the monotony, and the boredom. Redemption came from accepting all of it as the grace and rhythm of nature, rather than wasting mental energy longing for the thaw.

This challenging lesson took me a long, long time to embody. I had so much internal resistance, so much needing to control the situation. But what folly for man to think that he can control nature! When that realization finally sank in during my fifth winter, it was like emancipation. An enormous relief. *I'm not in control!* It landed like an epiphany in my mind. *I was never in control.* I released even the lingering despair I still clung to over my part in the tragic death of Comrade Rosa.

When the thaw arrived that year, it actually surprised me. It was "unexpected" and felt like a true miracle—that nature could rebuild itself after so much death! Miracles abounded everywhere that spring. Every new leaf, the song of birds, chatter of chipmunks. I felt giddy—like Adam, exploring the Garden of Eden.

But then, inevitably, the mind would come back—*Where was my Eve?*

And once again I found myself longing for something that wasn't present.

Where was Comrade Rosa? I wondered. *Is there life after death? Or does it all end in a bleak void, like the cruel Siberian winters?* I longed for some reassurance. Then, on June 30, 1908, I experienced something I will never forget.

It was early morning, perhaps 7 a.m., when I left the cabin to go fishing in the stream. The woods were buzzing with insects, birds, and scurrying squirrels. But everything stopped suddenly. There was a moment of dead quiet. It was bizarre—even foreboding.

I looked up at the sky and saw something that made no sense. A fiery streak of blazing light, slashing from the heavens to the distant horizon, like a cannonball from G-d that split the sky in two and filled it with fire. I was engulfed in an instantaneous heat wave, along with a rush of violent wind that blew me off my feet. Trees were uprooted, and animals scrambled in every direction.

Then, moments later, came a thunderous, booming explosion that shook the earth and sent clouds of dust across the entire sky, obscuring the sunlight and turning day into night. I was stupefied. It felt like the end of the world.

I stumbled back to check on Sarnai and the other villagers. Physically shaken, but uninjured, we huddled together not knowing if more terror from the sky would be raining down on us. The enormousness of what had happened left me in both awe and panic. Slowly, as the dust settled, things began to return to normal. But even Sarnai had no words of wisdom to impart.

After several days of agitation and confusion, word began to filter out. The sheriff delivered reports of the cataclysmic impact of a heavenly body a few hundred miles north of us. One of the countless flashing stars that streaked across our cloudless evening sky apparently crashed in Tunguska. Many decades later, I'd learn that the so-called "Tunguska Event" had been the largest meteoric impact on earth in recorded history. Despite destroying millions of trees, remarkably, perhaps miraculously, the meteor claimed only three lives. Even though I couldn't begin to comprehend the full magnitude of the event at the time, it occurred to me that had the meteor's trajectory been ever-so-slightly different, we could all have been wiped out in an instant. And I began, once again, to feel blessed. Why worry about things we cannot control? As Sarnai would say, "enjoy the miracle one day at a time." And I did. I tried.

But that, too, would soon change.

Some months later, I realized that mental states themselves change like the seasons—my mood once again became subdued. Leaves were falling to the ground as we headed into another winter. This one was perhaps the worst.

The cold weather invariably posed challenges to my health. Even though my tonsils had been removed, the precipitous and sudden drop in temperatures could bring sniffles or a cough, and sometimes a fever, which would dampen my already bleak mood. There's no greater way to douse one's hope than when seeds of doubt are planted in one's mind. Doubt can destroy everything.

I succumbed to this more than once. And one time—during the sixth winter of my exile—it nearly destroyed me. I had contracted a terrible fever that year, and it was causing hallucinations and paranoia. Bedridden and weak, I yearned to clutch my precious carved rose, which had always brought me comfort. But, alarmingly, it was nowhere to be found.

In my paranoia, I began to believe that Sarnai had stolen it—that she was, in actuality, a witch working for the Romanovs, like the evil Rasputin (who was also from Siberia). So convinced was I of her malevolent intent that I refused to let Sarnai treat me this time, and my fever got considerably worse. My teeth would chatter with chills and I would gather all my blankets, only to toss them off moments later, when my insides felt like a boiling cauldron. This continued for days.

Then came the doubt—deep and insidious.

I began second-guessing everything that had happened to me, reinterpreting it in the worst possible light. I started to believe that everyone around me had a nefarious agenda. I thought back to my encounter with Minne in Krasnoyarsk, when she'd told me that she'd heard that my family had made it to America. What if Minne had been lying? She needed an accomplice for her escape plan from the hospital. What if she fabricated the news about my family simply in order to recruit my assistance?

It suddenly made perfect sense. I'd been duped. My family was dead. Just like Comrade Rosa—which meant there was no longer any reason for me to continue.

With these heavy thoughts infecting my mind like a cancer, I rose slowly from my bed one night. With a great emptiness in my heart, I wandered out into the moonlight, trudging away from Sarnai's cabin into the woods.

Wind whistled around me. The snow was thick.

I found a clearing and lay down, staring up at the godless sky, as snow fell all around me. With temperatures below freezing, it was only a matter of minutes before hypothermia would take hold, slowing my pulse and circulation, and then stopping my breath...

I closed my eyes. Prepared to end it.

Then—I had this sudden feeling that there was a "Presence." A force that was all around me. I opened my eyes and gasped.

My beloved mother was there in the woods with me! Clear as day. Standing over me with a beatific smile, under the falling snow. She didn't say a word. But her presence conveyed volumes.

With her right hand, she beckoned me—"come." Then the vision vanished in the moonlight. I sprang up from the snow with newfound conviction. My mother was alive, no doubt about it. She was safe in the West with the rest of my family.

And so another heavenly body lit a line across my sky, shook the earth, and swept me off my feet. But this light turned what could have been an endless night into a lasting dawn.

My job was to survive Siberia. And join them.

PART II

THE WEST

CHAPTER 17

COMRADES EVERYWHERE

You cannot begin to imagine the overwhelming rapture that I felt on the morning of July 7, 1913, when I awoke to a roaring sound that shook the slumbering village.

Emerging from Sarnai's cabin in the woods to crickets everywhere and a gentle breeze, I beheld something I had never seen—a bicycle without pedals that made puffs of smoke like a locomotive as it appeared to move magically on its own!

Known as a "motorcycle," I had never seen one before. This particular model was a Gottlieb Daimler from Germany. Many years later I was told that the Russian authorities had purchased a fleet of them, for long-distance voyages and couriers.

"Rakow, Yosef?" the courier called out. I nodded.

"I have papers authorizing your release," he held up another item that was new to me—a stiff board with a metal clasp, used to secure documents (a "clipboard").

Marveling at how the world had changed in my ten years of hibernation, my face became flushed with joy as I took in my new reality: I was free!

It was difficult to say goodbye to my little village and the Kaldaens who had become like family to me, especially Sarnai, without whom I would not have survived. Her wrinkled eyes became moist, like mine, as she embraced me. Having helped me find my carved rose, Sarnai now handed it to me solemnly.

She placed the carving into my open palms and curled them closed around it, along with her own. We clasped the rose talisman within our four hands and gazed quietly at each other. The moment was deeply symbolic—for her name, in Mongolian, also meant "rose." Sarnai was asking me to take her with me—in my heart.

I felt a lump in my throat. Feeling overwhelmed herself, Sarnai turned and quietly walked into the woods.

I collected my clothing and other belongings, including the two items that were as precious to me as my carved wooden rose—my mother's pearl earring and my journal.

Then, with a final wave to Batu, Arban, Sheriff Brukhanov, and the other villagers, I climbed aboard the seat attached to the motorcycle, known as the "sidecar," and off we roared.

The roads had been improved since I had taken this route on horseback with Arban, nine years earlier—and, by nightfall, we had reached Krasnoyarsk. The motorcycle courier drove me to the military garrison, where I was given a cot for the night, along with a ticket on the morning's train to return to Pinsk. It took me a moment to register the incredible news: I was going home!

After a fitful night's sleep, replete with comical, recurring nightmares of missing the train, again and again, I awoke, finally, and walked myself to the Krasnoyarsk train station, where a gendarme checked my ticket and transfer papers, then waved me with a yawn onto the platform. Bursting with exuberance, I joyously boarded the train, where I sat and gazed through the window. Everything looked magnificent and pastoral. A large flock of sheep grazed in the distant pasture, where a hunting dog stood near a tree, his snout pointed toward the sky, barking raucously.

The locomotive let out a deep sigh; the wheels began to turn. Impulsively, without thinking, I quietly said to myself: "Long live the universal freedom of oppressed races and masses in all nationalities across the entire world!"

The train engineer, his whistle sounding in the air, gave a shout, and steam from the train's flues wove white banners across the sky. Watching fields and forests go by in their hypnotic rhythm, I was powerless to keep from falling asleep.

When I awoke from my long sleep the next day, the train's humming told me that I was in Tomsk. Through the train's window, I watched two roosters with colored feathers in a pitched battle. A yellow goat came running up and chased the battling cocks apart. Taking a hunk of black bread that I was given at the garrison, I began to chew and enjoy the fresh air of my long-awaited freedom.

The railroad, like the roadways, had been greatly improved in my absence, without any breaks in the line. Within a week and quite miraculously, I was home in Pinsk.

As I exited the Pinsk train station, I realized right away that the city had gotten bigger, with far more people in the streets. I spotted my first automobile—or "horseless carriage," as some people still called them—and I was immediately amused by the violent sound of its klaxon horn that warned pedestrians to get out of the way. There appeared to be a new park across from the depot, featuring a pigeon-strewn statue of Tsar Nicholas on horseback—which reminded me to stay focused on the mission at hand.

While I was now free from captivity, I was still not free to travel abroad. I could not leave Russia without an official passport bearing the tsar's imperial seal.

So I headed, at once, for Brestskiy Lane, where my siblings had told me to find the forger, Chaim Lescher. It was a short walk along the river and then the first left just before the bridge. But, as I went to cross the boulevard, I was almost trampled by a pair of mounted Cossack guards, galloping by in a hurry. I leapt back in alarm.

It was a reminder to stay vigilant. Even though I was not currently a suspect, tensions between the Romanov regime and the revolutionary movement remained high. I could certainly be rearrested. So I looked carefully in both directions, this time, before turning onto Brestskiy Lane, a smaller residential street lined with birch trees.

"Last house at the end of the lane" was what I recalled Max telling me. But which side? To the left was a building with three stories; to the right, a more modest dwelling. I chose right. A forger would keep a low profile.

Checking again that no one was watching, I moved up to the door and knocked.

There was no response. I knocked again—and waited. I noticed that the porch was covered in cobwebs and debris. Perhaps Lescher no longer lived here. Then I saw a face in the window to the left—a little girl who'd been silently observing me.

"I'm looking for Chaim Lescher," I said. "Is he here?"

The girl gazed at me with troubled eyes. She seemed to be about twelve years old. The door opened suddenly, as if of its own accord. I stepped into the dark vestibule, strewn with trash. A mouse scurried into the corner. I turned to see the girl aiming a gun at me.

"Who are you?" she asked, cocking the hammer to shoot.

I raised my arms and quickly recounted my story of being arrested as my family fled and serving ten years in Siberian exile for revolutionary activities. She nodded, apparently satisfied with my response, and lowered the gun.

"Welcome, Comrade," she said with a graveness that belied her age. "How can I help you?"

I told her of my desperation to go to the West and be reunited with my family. I needed travel papers—that's why I had come to see Lescher.

"Chaim Lescher is dead," she said quietly.

The girl registered the bitter disappointment in my face; she asked if I had any money. I admitted that I did not, and I began to realize the true hope-lessness of my plight. In the optimism surrounding my release, I had allowed myself to indulge in fantasies of a happy future. I had imagined a joyous seder meal in America alongside mother, Sonya, and Max, with Father leading us in the observances. That vision shattered suddenly before my eyes as I stared at this toughened girl, who was clearly as broken as I was.

"Come back tomorrow at noon," she said after a moment.

Given the balmy summer temperatures in Pinsk, I decided to sleep outdoors that night in the public park. For breakfast, I snuck into the alleyway behind the home of a city official, who had a garden with ripe strawberries. Then I bided my time until the appointed hour of midday, when I returned promptly to the forger's house, wondering what was in store for me.

The girl, much friendlier this time, handed me an envelope. Inside, I found travel documents, which were slightly off—the typography somewhat imperfect, the seal smudged.

"Who forged this?" I asked.

She had done it herself, she explained proudly. Her father had been training her as an apprentice before he died. She was an orphan now—and clearly quite lonely. She felt sympathy for my predicament and wanted to help. Not only did she decline payment for her work, she actually gave me twenty rubles for my journey.

I was deeply touched. Her generosity and understanding were just the beginning of numerous acts of kindness I received from strangers along my voyage—comrades who were sympathetic to the cause.

Just as I was leaving the company of this extraordinary girl, she eyed my clothing, which was old and stained. Thinking it might arouse suspicion, she offered to provide me with a fresh set of clothes from the closet of her late father, who was about my size. In fact, his clothes fit me perfectly. And, when I went to pull on his pants, I had another experience of a new invention that was unfamiliar to me—a zipper!

All the pants that I had known had buttons on the fly. And here was this new-fangled way of uniting the two sides. I marveled at its ingenious efficiency. In a curious way, the manner in which the zipper brought two sides together so effortlessly mirrored my desire to be reunited expeditiously with my family.

As I entered the now-familiar Pinsk train depot, I checked the platform for the presence of police, but none were present, thankfully. I took a breath and approached the westbound train. I could only afford a ticket to the first town in Austria, which was Brod, where I'd spent time during my self-imposed first exile.

I handed my paperwork to the conductor and waited. Would it pass muster? He eyed me while checking the slightly smudged imperial stamp on my passport. I tried to remain calm. The official snorted, smoothed out his whiskers, then handed the document back to me, unceremoniously, and moved on. I breathed a sigh of relief and darted onto the train.

Then, with a whistle that must have reverberated across my hometown, the locomotive screeched to life suddenly and we rumbled to my destiny.

I can hardly describe the joy I felt as we rolled freely, several hours later, across the frontier that I had previously only crossed illegally. What a feeling!

My voyage across Europe was filled with memorable encounters. Revolutionary fervor had begun to sweep the continent, so everywhere I went I was treated as a "true Bolshevik" who had suffered greatly under tsarist tyranny. People provided me with shelter and food, and I did odd construction jobs here and there to earn some cash. My ear for language came in handy, and I found I picked up a few words quite quickly and managed to be understood.

My goal was to reach England, where I could catch a steamship across the Atlantic. With tensions growing as the nations of Europe prepared to enter the Great War, I decided to leave Austria as quickly as I could and avoid Germany altogether. My plan was to stop in Switzerland, which had always been neutral, then go to France and cross the English Channel to get to Great Britain.

In each of these countries, I met socialist sympathizers of great renown, though I wasn't aware, at the time, that they were famous. Central to revolutionary thinking was the notion that all comrades were of equal stature in the movement: brothers and sisters in the revolt against tyranny. It was exciting—and inspiring.

The first of these celebrity encounters occurred in Zürich, which had become a hotbed for European socialists. It was also a center for the suffragette movement.

Women had recently won the right to vote in Finland and Norway. Now they were organizing in other countries such as Switzerland. On the day I arrived in Zürich, I found out from some comrades who befriended me at the train station that there was a party that evening to discuss the issue of women's rights, and they invited me to tag along with them.

It was at a nice apartment on Universitätsrasse near the University of Zürich.

There were many students and professors in attendance. I was told that the place belonged to a hero of European Marxists named Rosa Luxemburg, one of the first women to be awarded a doctorate in Law. While unassuming in terms of appearance, Professor Luxemburg, who cradled a Persian cat in her arms, was very much holding court in the salon amongst her fawning students, many of whom were female.

There was another professor who also caught my eye: an eccentric man with wild hair who seemed to be obsessed with the globe in the library, which he spun again and again, fixated on its movement, deep in thought. I watched him for quite some time, intrigued by what might be going through his mind.

"He's in the department of Theoretical Physics," said the male comrade who had invited me to the party.

Many years later, I realized who this man was: Albert Einstein, a lifelong socialist. I also learned that our hostess, Rosa Luxemburg, was eventually assassinated for her radical views by authorities in Germany.

When I arrived in Paris, one week later, it happened again.

I met some bohemians who were going to an art opening at 25 rue Victor-Massé, a gallery belonging to a Jewish dealer named Berth Weill—another staunch socialist who was known for championing young, avant-garde artists. When we arrived just after 10 p.m., it was quite a scene. The Paris intelligentsia was out in numbers. Lively music emanated from a gramophone—a device I had heard about but never actually seen until that moment. I was intrigued by the spinning wax disc and how it was magically producing this entrancing music. Some couples were dancing, but the place was so crowded that they had spilled out into the street. Paris was in the midst of a heat wave, so some of the young men had removed their shirts. They were passing around a bottle of absinthe and howling revolutionary slogans. One of them had chiseled cheekbones and dark, intense eyes. They were calling him "the Spaniard."

It was Pablo Picasso, another brother in the revolution.

While I had no direct interactions with Picasso or Einstein, when I crossed the English Channel and made my way to London, I met a professor who took a specific interest in my story. It began when I stumbled upon a political rally in Trafalgar Square. It was September 21, 1913, the fall equinox, which fell that year on a Sunday. The gathering was not terribly well attended, fifty or sixty people in all. But they were vocal and very passionate about socialism, pacifism, and anti-imperialism—which were intricately intertwined in their view. In war, it was always the disenfranchised and poor that did the fighting and died disproportionately on behalf of the powerful and their imperial agendas.

As I listened to their speeches using my limited English and trying my best to follow, I was approached by a young, bearded fellow who slapped me on the back and asked: "Russki?" He must have recognized me as a fellow countryman from the Russian cap that I wore with its glistening visor. His name was Ivan. I was elated to meet someone who spoke my language. Ivan peppered me with questions, and I relayed my saga of joining the revolutionary movement at age fifteen, then being separated from my family and sentenced to ten years of exile in Siberia. He was entranced.

"You must meet the professor," he declared suddenly and led me to the small stage where a distinguished-looking gentleman in his forties was wrapping up a speech, pounding the podium with his fist as he made his impassioned arguments. There was raucous applause as the esteemed pundit concluded his remarks—he was clearly beloved by all in attendance. Ivan intercepted the man as he descended from the platform and introduced me as a "Bolshevik hero" from the motherland. The professor seemed fascinated. It was Bertrand Russell, mathematician, philosopher, and historian, who taught as a lecturer at Trinity College, Cambridge, where he had gone to school.

As we stood, surrounded by pigeons beneath Nelson's grandiose column in the center of the square, Professor Russell instigated a series of questions, which Ivan translated, and I answered dutifully. He was intensely curious about the working conditions in tsarist Russia. When I recounted my horrific experience in the match factory, Professor Russell insisted that I return to Cambridge with him to speak directly to his students. Flattered and honored by the offer, I ended up staying in Cambridge for two weeks as the professor's guest.

It was an unforgettable experience to spend time on the majestic, centuries-old campus. While it was ostensibly a haven for England's elite, Professor Russell's students were in open rebellion against the status quo. Every evening after classes, we'd gather in his quarters to debate the issues of the day. It was enthralling for me—a condensed taste of the education I'd so yearned for in those years of exile.

Professor Russell was deeply supportive of my plans to go to America.

"The Yankees need a real revolutionary like you," he smiled, between sips of sherry and puffs of his pipe. Professor Russell kindly offered to pay for my steamship ticket. He also gave me a book that would become my bible for the next three months: a Russian-English dictionary.

"You're a brave man," said Ivan, joking about the fact that I would be travelling to America on a boat. (The Titanic had sunk the year before!)

Chapter 18

Finding Your People

"I hereby declare, on oath, that I absolutely and entirely renounce and abjure all allegiance and fidelity to any foreign prince, potentate, state, or sovereignty, of whom or which I have heretofore been a subject or citizen."

The voices were strong. Almost 250, coming from sixty different countries. Every ethnicity, skin color, age, and religion was represented in the cavernous hall—a sea of elated immigrants waving their American flags, which fluttered like autumn leaves on a drift of Aspen trees. These soon-to-be citizens were teary-eyed as they faced the fifty-foot banner of the Stars and Stripes, suspended up front, along with a depiction of the Statue of Liberty and a photograph of then-president Barack Obama. The year was 2012.

Among the attendees of this particular Naturalization Ceremony, which took place at the Corpus Christi Federal Courthouse on January 2, was Patrizia Alvarado, who beamed proudly, clutching her flag, as she recited the "Oath of Allegiance" to the land she was now embracing.

Standing next to her and fighting hard to hold back tears was Enrique, whom Patti had married three years prior—setting her on the

Joseph Rakow

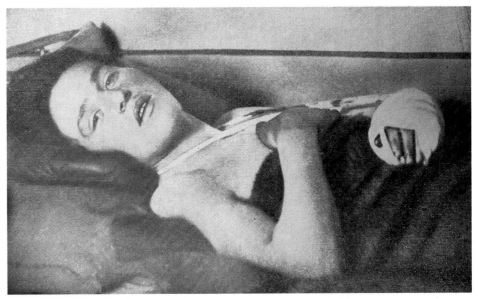

Joseph Rakow at the Pinsk hospital after being shot by police as he attempted to escape. He was only fifteen years old.

Joseph Rakow experiencing another Siberian winter (1910).

Rose Raff and Joseph Rakow were married in Chicago in 1919.

Joseph Rakow and his mother
Sophie in Chicago, circa 1928.

Joseph in Chicago (1950).

Rose, Joseph, and Saralie in Chicago (1950).

John's mom Saralie Rakow—Sullivan High School in Chicago, IL (1950).

John with his grandmother Rose Rakow in Rock Island, IL (1966).

John cut his teeth in political activism as a Student School Board member and President of the Rock Island High School Student Senate (1981).

John at Rock Island High School in 1982.

John is a proud graduate of Rock Island
High School (1982).

John moved to Los Angeles in 1986 to work for US Senator Alan Cranston.

At the age of twenty-eight, John was the youngest President of the Los Angeles Transportation Commission in history.

John delivers a speech in LA City Hall (1994).

Bill Clinton called it the "shot heard around the world" when Democrat Loretta Sanchez beat right-wing conservative Congressman "B1-Bob" Dornan in 1996.

The Shallmans with then Senator Barack Obama campaigning for President in Iowa (2007).

Shooting a political commercial with
Magic Johnson in Los Angeles (2013).

John pictured with California Senate
President Pro Tem Kevin de León in the
state capitol in Sacramento (2015).

John with Senator Isadore Hall and Assembly member Reginald Jones-Sawyer in
Los Angeles (2015).

John with his mom Saralie Rakow Shallman in Los Angeles (2016).

John's siblings and parents—Morty, Saralie, Bill, Dan, Debra, John, and Nancy in Santa Monica, CA (2018).

John with US Senator Elizabeth Warren (Massachusetts) in 2018.

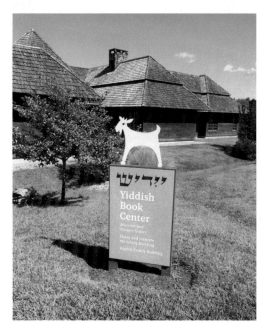

Whether it was divine intervention or simple
coincidence, John happened to drive by the
Yiddish Book Center in Amherst, MA while
visiting his daughter at Amherst College.
This "accident" led to the translation of his
grandfather's manuscript.

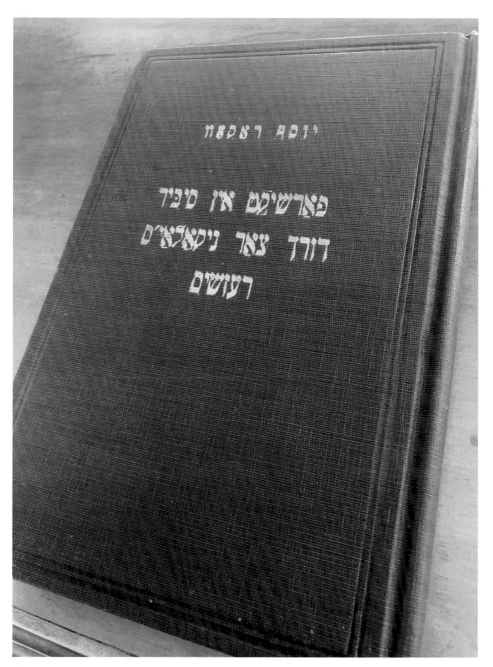

The Book—Joseph Rakow's Manuscript.

The Shallman Family—John, Lani, Ariana Rose, Nina Juliette, Benjamin Joseph, and Jonah Samuel.

path toward citizenship. Also flanking Patti on that momentous day was her daughter, Alexa, then eight and still innocent. As a minor, she was about to be naturalized, too, along with her mom.

Alexa's eyes darted around the hall in excitement, but she couldn't possibly fathom at her tender age the profound significance of what was about to transpire. Fortunately, Enrique's sister, Maria, who was also in attendance, had had the foresight to capture the ceremony on her cell phone. This precious recording is what John watched in rapt attention, along with his daughter, Juliette, who was home from college, during the summer of 2018.

Locating this footage had been Juliette's idea. Increasingly incensed by the polarizing tactics of the Trent campaign, she felt their vitriolic tone was one of the factors that had enabled the tragic shooting at Alexa's summer program, which Juliette could still barely think about without becoming enraged and overwhelmed by sadness. It was time to seize the narrative, she thought—offer the electorate a story of hope. That's when Juliette had the inspiration—surely there must be footage of Patti's citizenship ceremony?

She mentioned the idea to her dad, who appreciated the genius of it right away. He managed to secure the official house feed from the Corpus Christi Federal Courthouse. And then there was this footage from Maria's phone, which John and Juliette were now watching on the TV in his office. It was deeply moving. Patti looked radiant in a floral-patterned dress, her right palm raised solemnly, framed by her handsome husband and adorable daughter, as she continued the citizenship oath: "I will perform work of national importance…"

Like run for office, thought John and Juliette simultaneously, as if they were of one mind—both of them riveted by what was unfolding before them on the LCD monitor, where Alexa was looking up at her mom, as Patti concluded her oath: "I take this obligation freely, without any mental reservation or purpose of evasion; so help me G-d."

"Congratulations," said the presiding judge at the podium. "You are now citizens of the United States of America!" And that's when everyone in the room went nuts.

Enrique hugged his wife and then kissed her passionately. He grabbed Alexa, whom he'd adopted as his own daughter, and lifted her jubilantly onto his shoulders, where she waved a flag high above the crowd. It was picture perfect—you couldn't have scripted it any better. Even in Hollywood.

When Juliette had pitched her father the idea of using this footage for a political ad about reclaiming the American Dream—to take back the narrative that Ralph Trent had tainted for his own political ambitions—John had agreed. *Brilliant.*

Juliette had always functioned as a de facto consigliere to her father on various campaigns. She was a strong writer, with passion in spades and incredible instincts when it came to messaging. They went to work immediately on the spot. Juliette dug up some rousing music and drone shots of the Statue of Liberty, which helped drive the emotional crescendo, ending with a final title card:

THE AMERICAN DREAM
IT'S FOR IMMIGRANTS.

The spot tested off the charts with focus groups. Sure enough, after they began running it on the local airwaves, Patti finally cracked double-digits in the polls.

In sudden elation, John turned to his daughter and said: "Come work for me." Juliette smiled demurely. But her father was dead serious.

"You're fired!" barked Mark Dunham, Lani's bulldog boss at the Dunham & Grilley advertising agency. He did it in front of everybody. The entire office.

The object of his wrath was Melody Nahhas, the young intern on

Lani's team who had a neuroatypical profile, which made complex inter-personal outbursts highly confusing for her.

"What are you waiting for?" snapped Mark. "Get out! Your face makes me sick."

Melody gathered her belongings, desperately trying to make sense of the whirlwind of emotions that were hitting her faster than she could process them. Striving unsuccessfully not to cry, she headed in humil-iation toward the door of the conference room, where everyone had gathered for the weekly staff meeting.

Lani, who was going through her own whirlwind of emotions, decided on impulse to intervene. "Wait," she said softly to Melody. "You're not going anywhere."

It had suddenly become clear to her that this was a David and Goli-ath moment. And Lani—like her husband John—had a thing for under-dogs. It was one of the ways they had bonded. Maybe it was the fact that she was the daughter of immigrants: Lani's father, Celso, had been the ultimate underdog—born into extreme poverty in the Philippines and one of ten children, whose mother died giving birth to the youngest of them. Seeking a brighter future, he eventually joined the US Navy, where he served honorably for more than two decades, granting him the right, under the Nationality Act of 1940, to become a naturalized US citizen. He married his wife, Loreta, a Filipina from the Bicol region whom he met while back home on leave, and they raised four children in Amer-ica with dignity and poise. This upbringing is what gave Lani the moral compass to be able to speak truth to power, especially to egomaniacs like Mark Dunham.

So, with profound authority that surprised everyone, including her-self, Lani turned to her boss and said: "You and I need a sidebar."

"Oh, please," he rolled his eyes.

"Now!" insisted Lani.

Moments later they'd decamped into the corner office, where Mark crossed his arms and kicked his Gucci loafers onto the oversize desk—primarily used as a platform to display prized photos of him with Kanye West, Ronald Reagan, and other celebrities.

Lani said: "I don't appreciate how you handled that."

Mark shrugged. *Whatever.*

"If you want to fire someone on my team, it should come through me," Lani continued. "Besides, no one should lose their job over an idea."

"Her idea sucked!" sneered Mark. "Most idiotic concept I ever heard."

Lani was silent. She could not have disagreed more vehemently, which had her wondering: was this really her tribe?

Dunham & Grilley had been invited to submit publicity concepts for the Americana at Brand, an outdoor mall that featured an old-fashioned trolley car and a "dancing" fountain. While plenty of locals frequented the lively shopping plaza, the owners of the Americana were interested in figuring out ways to promote it as an "urban destination" for tourists.

The idea that Melody had proposed took inspiration from recent events in Egypt, where her father had been born. Just as Egyptians had drawn the attention of the world to Tahrir Square by posting a series of escalating cell phone videos during the Arab Spring, Melody thought they could create a social media campaign for the Americana driven by consumers, who'd be recruited and incentivized to post with increasing frequency until it felt like an "uprising."

Lani had no clue why this idea had caused her volatile boss to explode. She herself thought it was inspired. Perhaps it was the political connotations that spooked Mark. Whatever the reason, Lani was appalled by the way he had publicly shamed a poor girl who was just trying to do her job. Lani had specifically been encouraging risk taking among her team members to spark their creativity and out-of-the-box thinking, of which Melody's idea was a prime example. If anything, it should have been rewarded.

"Are we done?" Mark was getting antsy.

"We haven't even begun." She held her ground. The situation was becoming increasingly clear to her.

"*What?* I sure hope you don't expect a goddamn apology."

"I expect a lot more than that," she said with the calm conviction of someone who knows they're speaking truth to power. As Mark fidgeted with his fancy cigar cutter, Lani took a deep breath and said: "Melody gets her job back—or I walk with her."

Mark guffawed. "Yeah, right!"

Lani grinned right back at him. She'd been secretly pining for a moment like this. "Good-bye, asshole."

Mark stared in stunned silence as Lani spun on her heels and left.

After gathering her things in a banker's box, Lani joined Melody, who, carrying her own box, was holding the elevator for her former supervisor. They rode down in silence for a moment.

Melody was mortified. Her future appeared to be in shambles.

Lani, meanwhile, was feeling more and more certain about the next move. This was the opportunity she'd been seeking. For years, Lani had been yearning to hang her own shingle—getting away from toxic, patriarchal egomaniacs and finding like-minded people who shared her values and vision. One such individual was right next to her.

So, before reaching the lobby, Lani turned to Melody with a big smile and said: "Come work for me."

CHAPTER 19

LAND OF THE FREE

When I finally saw her, the feeling was overwhelming.

She was taller than I expected; her expression resolute, stoic, and unwavering. She appeared to be staring directly at me—of that I had no doubt. But I was hardly alone in my certainty. Indeed, a collective roar rose across all six decks of the immense steamship as it lumbered into New York harbor, its great horns bellowing as if exhaling a celebratory sigh, while thousands of immigrants ran to the ship's rails to get a good look at the magnificent colossus that greeted us. Each one of these hopeful souls felt (as I did) that Lady Liberty was here to welcome us individually and personally—like a long-lost mother. That feeling made up for all the suffering we had endured to make it here.

The transatlantic journey had been harrowing. I'd boarded the *RMS Lusitania* six days prior on September 23, 1913. Bertrand Russell's Russian assistant, Ivan, had been gracious enough to accompany me on the train from Cambridge to Liverpool to see me off at the docks. The ship was enormous, the largest man-made object I'd ever seen (other than the Eiffel Tower)—six decks all told, from the Saloon Deck, which accommodated 500 first-class passengers, down to the steerage quarters, where I'd be housed, along with 1,200 other immigrant hopefuls. The ticket, kindly paid for by Professor Russell, cost six pounds (about thirty dollars).

The *Lusitania* was certainly an impressive ship—fastest on the ocean at the time. Ivan explained to me that most third-class quarters on transatlantic liners consisted of cavernous dormitories, housing hundreds, with limited access to washrooms and no dedicated dining room. The *Lusitania* had us in rooms of six to eight, with a common cafeteria—practically palatial in comparison to the standards to which I'd grown accustomed in the Russian penal system. Professor Russell had chosen the *Lusitania* for that very reason; I was deeply touched by his kindness and support.

Waving to Ivan as the mighty steamship pulled away from its dock, I felt grateful and relieved to be finally sailing to America—a sentiment shared by all my fellow passengers, I assumed, since Europe was on the brink of monumental turmoil. The Great War would soon claim forty million lives. The very ship upon which we were sailing would be torpedoed off the coast of Ireland in 1915 by a German U-boat, causing it to sink within eighteen minutes and drowning two-thirds of its passengers.

While we were spared that level of tragedy, the crossing was still rough. Bad weather and choppy seas made the vessel teeter incessantly and yaw with unexpected violence, causing passengers, especially those below deck, to vomit on a daily basis. This exacerbated the spread of contagious diseases like typhoid and tuberculosis; almost half of the third-class passengers became sick. After an examination by the ship medic, who was clearly overworked, numerous individuals, even entire families, were taken away to designated quarantine areas. They'd continue to be detained until symptom-free upon arrival in America. Some passengers didn't even make it that far, perishing in limbo between the old world and the new. An elderly gentleman from Estonia, Matis Kask, who slept in the bunk across from me, died one night of a massive heart attack. His widow, Olga, was beside herself—as Jewish law requires that you bury your dead on the same day, because an unburied corpse, according to Devarim (Deuteronomy) "is a curse to G-d."

Ship Captain J. T. W. Charles, following maritime tradition, arranged to have Mr. Kask buried at sea, but this did little to comfort his poor widow. While obeying one Jewish law, she was now in violation of another, which requires a body to be interred in the soil. In her confusion and mourning, she found herself at a complete loss. I can still see Mrs. Kask, wailing inconsolably as we all stood by and watched her husband's body fall several stories from the steerage deck and disappear with a foreboding splash into the cold, gray Atlantic.

The somber incident put a pall on the already dampened mood we were all experiencing in the dark quarters within the bowels of the ship, which, while more accommodating than prior vessels, was nonetheless still hellish. Rats roamed freely, along with the ticks and lice that fed on them—all of these potential vectors and carriers of disease. Indeed, the passing of Matis Kask was hardly the only death amongst the steerage passengers. Numerous children died, even babies.

With so much coughing around me, I did my best to keep my distance and bide my time. I thought of my dear sister, Sonya, and her fragile lungs, hoping that she'd received the medical care she so desperately needed in America.

You can't imagine my feeling of relief and exaltation when I awoke on the fifth night to the sound of screaming and running feet.

"Land ahoy!" people were shouting.

I leapt out of my bunk and ran out onto the foredeck, where it was still dark.

Everyone was crowding at the bow and staring toward a distant beacon. A lighthouse!

"That's Nantucket!" shouted a giddy Italian named Enzo, who knew a thing or two about American geography. Enzo explained in excitement that Nantucket was an island off the coast of Massachusetts, which meant we would soon be sailing past Long Island. Everyone stayed on deck, foregoing further sleep, in jubilant anticipation of seeing our soon-to-be homeland.

Before we knew it, more lighthouses appeared, flickering in the distance.

But it didn't make any sense. There must have been thousands of them. Then it became clear—these were not lighthouses, but illumination from New York itself, which had installed 37,000 electrical streetlights by 1913. I had never seen so much light in the dead of night. "They call it the city that never sleeps," mused Enzo.

By morning, with glorious pink skies and seagulls swooping above, we came upon the New York skyline, which had me shake my head in awe. There they were—the "skyscrapers" that Max had told me about—buildings so tall that they literally scratched at the heavens! I could not fathom the feats of engineering that would be required to erect these colossal towers.

Before landing in New York, we stopped at a checkpoint off the coast of Staten Island where doctors came aboard, inspecting us one by one for dangerous communicable diseases such as smallpox, yellow fever, plague, cholera, and leprosy. Many were pulled aside and forced to disembark. They'd be held for months, if necessary, in a quarantine facility.

Then, at long last, we sailed into New York harbor with its majestic Statue of Liberty—a sight I will never forget.

While the ship's course was not quite close enough for me to read the famous poem inscribed on a plaque on the statue's base, I learned the powerful words by Emma Lazarus upon our arrival at Ellis Island:

Give me your tired, your poor,
Your huddled masses yearning to breathe free…

I would later read that Miss Lazarus, a fifth-generation American from a very wealthy family with Sephardic roots, had composed her poem specifically for Jews, like myself, fleeing pogroms in Russia. We were arriving by the thousands.

When we disembarked on Ellis Island, we were ushered into an enormous gallery with long lines and uniformed officials holding whistles and clipboards—shouting orders at us in English, which many of the arrivals did not understand. A second ship had arrived from Hamburg (the port my family had sailed from), which meant there were close to four thousand people inside the massive intake hall—daunting, to say the least, especially for someone traveling alone like myself. And I was in my twenties; there were plenty of unaccompanied minors, as young as nine or ten, who looked intimidated and bewildered.

As authorities whisked the first- and second-class passengers through the hall without a fuss, the rest of us were separated into two lines: one for women and children, the other for men. But this final inspection was simply a formality. No passports or visas were necessary in 1913 for entry into the United States—in fact, no papers were required at all. It was a paperless period. I had given my name verbally to the Purser as I boarded the *Lusitania* in Liverpool, and it had been duly entered into the ship manifest, which is what the New York authorities were now using to take an inventory of arriving passengers. When the official called out "Rakow, Joseph," I stepped forward in excitement and lifted my suitcase onto the table. He gave it a cursory inspection for contraband, then asked: "Age?"

"Twenty-five," I declared proudly in my rapidly improving English, having spent nearly every free moment of the last month scrutinizing page by page the Russian-English dictionary given to me in Cambridge by Professor Russell.

"Hometown?" he continued, filling out my arrival paperwork.

"Pinsk," I responded. He stamped the document, handed it over, and waved me through. But I wasn't quite ready to go. Looking beseechingly at the official, I asked: "You help me find my family?"

He stared back at me. "Your family's here in America?"

I nodded. "But you've got no clue where they are," he surmised. "They arrived here at Ellis Island like you?" he asked. I nodded.

"Lower East Side," he said empathically. "That's where all Russian Jews end up."

I left the hall in a state of euphoria with the knowledge that, after a decade of separation, I'd soon be reunited with my beloved family. Boarding one of the tugboats that took us in batches from Ellis Island to Battery Park, I inhaled the fresh, briny air and gazed up at the skyline in anticipation.

But as I stepped off the ferry and began to walk the streets of Lower Manhattan, I felt a vague sense of unease. The Lower East Side was where I'd find my family, according to the Ellis Island official. But surely, they couldn't be living here amongst these sterile streets with their cold towers of polished stone? Then I realized these were banks and financial institutions—it was Wall Street, where money and power were concentrated in the hands of the wealthiest Americans, such as the Morgans, Mellons, and Carnegies. Those "Robber Barons" that Professor Russell had warned me about.

Just one mile north, the city's character changed altogether. Bustling streets full of people and life, warm brick brownstones and apartments whose lower floors were lined with canopied shops selling felt hats, watches, and leather shoes. There were pushcarts overflowing with fresh produce and kosher meats. The abundance was extraordinary. And, even more extraordinary—everyone was speaking Yiddish!

My heart leapt for joy. It felt like I was home. Or a place that was even better than home. A place with plentiful food and prosperity for all, where people roamed freely without fear, where happiness quite literally filled the air. You could feel it.

I walked up to a vendor who was selling apples on a stick, covered in some kind of shiny coating. "Candied apples!" he shouted.

"I take one," I said curiously, then handed him some kopeks, which he accepted with a smile.

"You'll have to change your rubles for dollars," he said. "Go to Moshe Segal, on the corner of Grand and Montgomery. You can trust him."

"You know Avrom Rakow from Pinsk?" I asked hopefully.

It didn't register, so I added: "Married to Sophie Rakow. Father of Sonya and Max."

He shrugged. "What street are they on?"

"I don't know. That's why I ask."

"They arrived before you?" He was beginning to get the picture. "How long ago?"

"Ten years," I responded cheerfully, biting into the apple, which was so sweet it made me salivate. He stared at me grimly for a moment.

"Do you know how many Jews from Russia live in New York?"

I shook my head.

"One million." He said it softly, knowing it would be like a knife in my heart. My expression dropped. *One million?*

The apple vendor looked at me with compassion. "First day off the boat?"

I nodded, trying hard to keep from crying. He sighed, then pulled a coin out of his pocket—an American nickel. "Have you ever been to a Nickelodeon?"

My expression was blank. "They're everywhere," he said, handing me his coin. "My favorite is Fox's Dewey Theater in Union Square—one mile north." He pointed to Bowery Street. "It'll cheer you up. Guaranteed."

As I walked disconsolately after a very long day up Manhattan's oldest thoroughfare, the sun was just beginning to set, which brought a new kind of magic to the "city that never sleeps"—as streetlights came to life and automobile headlamps zipped along the avenues. By the time I reached Union Square, it was so bright it seemed like daytime. The Dewey was just one of eight "Nickelodeons" lining the square, with garish illuminated marquees. I still had no idea what these establishments had to offer exactly, but I was certainly curious to find out—a circus perhaps?

I crossed the plaza to approach the Dewey, which was owned by William Fox; his name ran prominently across its marquee. I'd later learn that he was a well-known resident of the Lower East Side who'd emigrated from Hungary as Vilmos Fuchs and would go on to found Fox Film Corporation (later named 20th Century Fox). On that breezy night in late September, I paid my five cents and was admitted into Mr. Fox's impressive establishment, which appeared to have the size and scale of an opera house. The theater itself was vast, the largest I'd ever seen—at least a thousand seats, most of which were filled. Yet, as the lights dimmed and the curtains opened, I was surprised to see no actual stage behind the parting drapes, but a flat white wall, instead.

Then, suddenly, the magic began: phosphorescent pictures appeared on that white wall—pictures that moved! People coming and going, horses, gun-fire, romance! I became entranced. Just as the apple seller had predicted, I was buoyed by the spectacle and left the theater in a much better mood. But as I watched other members of the audience going off in groups—laughing couples, smiling families, happy friends—my isolation hit me even harder than before. To make matters worse, it began to rain.

I wandered the streets, looking for a place where I could take shelter, when something unexpected caught my eye—a synagogue.

I couldn't remember the last time I'd stepped inside a temple of worship. Was it when I had taken the Bimah at my own bar mitzvah as a boy in Pinsk? It certainly must have been long before my time as a member of the Revolu-tionary Maximalists—since the movement disdained organized religion as a tool of the oppressors.

But that was all behind me now. I felt compelled to go inside and won-dered if it would be open at this late hour. Thankfully, I found a side door that was unlocked and let myself into the darkened synagogue. There was no one around.

I felt so alone—even lonelier, perhaps, than during my desolation in Siberia. For, having crossed half the world, I was still no closer to finding my family. It was beyond disheartening. I thought of my kind mother, who had appeared to me in a vision at my lowest point as snow fell around me in the Siberian woods. Where was she? Now that I needed her so desperately. *Where?*

For the first time since childhood, I fell to my knees and prayed.

Chapter 20

Torn Apart

Raising open palms to their ears, they chanted in perfect unison: "*Allaahu Akbar.*" (G-d is the Greatest.)

Moving as one, they bowed together, dropped to their knees, and prostrated their foreheads upon the small, unglazed disc placed on the rug before each congregant—the turbah, made of clay to represent the earth and symbolize that all men will one day return to the dust from which they emerged.

"*Subhaana Rabbi Al-A'laa wa Bihamdihi.*" (Glory be to my Exalted Lord; praise belongs to Him.)

This was recited just once in the sujud position, with both palms in contact with the earth, along with the forehead. Then, sitting up again, palms down on kneeling thighs, another: "*Allaahu Akbar.*"

The solemn prayer sequence continued, step by step, in perfect synchronization at the IMAN Foundation Mosque on Motor Avenue, just south of the (recently renamed) Twenty-First Century Fox. The beauty of this practice was that not only did the two hundred men gathered here for fajr (dawn prayers) feel deeply attuned to one another, they also felt connected to Muslims everywhere, some two billion people, who were worshiping across the world, using this precise prayer sequence, in a tradition going back 1,400 years. Same words, same vibration, emanating from faithful hearts in mosques and prayer rooms across lands and centuries—over a quadrillion times, if you did the math. That's what made the ritual so appealing to Bijan Yadzani, Rose's Persian boyfriend (who was still awaiting a response to his unexpected proposal of marriage). Praying the fajr helped Bijan sense his place in the universe.

Bijan was here with his father, Farshid. Ever since moving to Los Angeles, they'd been coming together to the mandatory first prayer every Friday at IMAN—an acronym for "Iranian-American Muslim Association of North America." In addition to being a mosque, IMAN was also a cultural center, which served, according to the website, "as a wonderful bridge between our glorious past and a future full of hope, an abode full of love and affection." Bijan appreciated their commitment to ecumenism and cooperation between all religions. He loved that there were Jewish texts in the bookstore, reminding him of the numerous connections between Sh'ia Islam and Judaism, such as the fact that both prescribed prayers to be performed three times a day—as opposed to the dominant Sunni branch of Islam, which insisted on five. Ninety percent of Muslims worldwide were Sunnis; the remaining ten percent, located mostly in Iran, were Shiites. And there were tensions between the sects, even violence at times, which troubled Bijan.

One of the reasons the young student of philosophy felt so drawn to the congregation at IMAN was its embrace of different viewpoints. Bijan's first experience at the cultural center had been attending a presentation by Younus Algohar, a peace activist and spiritual leader devoted to tolerance, divine love, and interfaith harmony. The talk had impressed Bijan deeply.

"Initially, all humanity was one," began Algohar, "when God created Adam and Eve, there were no differences. They were all brothers and sisters to each other. With the passage of time, when God introduced more prophets, one after the other, we happened to be diversified. We were divided into many different religions and races. With a widespread progeny of Adam, languages evolved, differences increased to a point where now, we have forgotten that we are the creation of the same God.

"On one side of the story, we have become so scientifically advanced. We have set our foot on the Moon and we are thinking about going to Mars. On the other hand, spiritually, we have become so shallow-witted. We cannot see that everybody is calling upon the same God with different names. Whether it is Ram, Wahe Guru, Bhagwan, Elohim, Yahweh, or God."[1]

Bijan nodded in vigorous agreement, exchanging a glance with his father, who had invited him to the talk. Afterward, they went for Cuban food at Versailles on Venice Boulevard and discussed the two subjects people are told never to raise over food: politics and religion. But these particular "taboos" were like catnip, or even crack, to the Yadzani boys.

"Karl Marx had it all wrong," Bijan dived right in. "Religion isn't the 'opium of the people.' It doesn't numb us from the truth of who we are. Quite the opposite—it's where we're all equal, which is why it should go hand in hand with socialism."

Farshid sipped his tea, smiling at his engaged son, who never failed to impress him.

"You're right," said the Sufi scholar. "And Marx would agree with you. That quote is always taken out of context. It begins with 'Religion is the sigh of the oppressed creature, the heart of a heartless world, and the soul of soulless conditions'—meaning it's the only place many of us can turn for refuge, when facing injustice that can't be cured."

Bijan listened attentively, as his learned father continued: "Take Islam, for instance. In our ritual prayers each individual Muslim is in direct contact with Allah. There is no need of a priest as an intermediary. It is a deeply individual practice. And yet, at the same time, we sacrifice our individuality to pray in lockstep with our neighbor and all the others in

---

1 Younus Algohar, "Kindle the Flame of Love—Iman Center, Los Angeles, USA," August 27, 2019. https://www.younusalgohar.net/articles/kindle-the-flame-of-love -iman-center-los-angeles-usa/.

the mosque—like ants toiling in unison to be of service to the colony's greater purpose. Selflessness is what makes it transcendent."

"Both individual and without identity at the same time." Bijan was starting to get it. Farshid nodded. *Exactly.* "The micro and the macro," his son continued. "That's why the Salaat prayers are so powerful."

Farshid's eyes wrinkled as he smiled in obvious pride. They decided to make dawn prayers on Friday a weekly ritual, which meant getting up as early as 4:30 a.m. during the summer months. But Bijan loved it. Many Southern California twenty-somethings set their alarms at that ungodly hour to hang with their surfboards and commune with the ocean—he did it to hang with his dad and commune with the universe.

"*Allaahu Akbar.*"

They raised their palms to their ears, along with Muslims everywhere. It made Bijan so happy.

After prayers, their weekly ritual always included breakfast, and Bijan was really looking forward to it on this particular Friday in August 2018. But it was not meant to be.

As the Yadzanis emerged from the IMAN mosque, they were met in the parking lot by four men in dark suits. "Farshid Yadzani, Bijan Yadzani," said one of them. "You need to come with us."

Bijan looked at his father in horror—were they being arrested?

Rose Simon sat on a stool in her studio, doing something she dreaded—but knew to be a necessary evil. Self-promotion. No career was possible these days without it, especially as an artist. So, Rose did what she had to do—took selfies as she painted, documented behind the scenes, and posted photographs of the works themselves, coupled with comments designed to provoke and engage her Instagram audience, which was small but growing. Bijan, of course, was her biggest fan.

When she had posted her favorite painting in the hammer-and-sickle series, writing "Capitalism is Evil!" he'd hearted it within seconds.

Neither of them could have possibly imagined the dire madness that would soon ensue. She got the call from Bijan at 9:20 a.m.

"I thought we were going to hike," she said. "Where are you?"

"I'm at LAX." His voice was trembling. "I'm being deported!"

"*What?*" She practically spat it out. "What about your parents?"

"They're here with me. We're being sent back to Iran."

Rose couldn't believe what she was hearing.

The men who'd intercepted Bijan and his father outside the mosque were Homeland Security agents. They'd loaded the professor and his son into a waiting SUV and driven them straight to the airport, where Farshid's wife, Esta, was already being detained—without even extending the courtesy of allowing the family to stop at their apartment to let them gather personal belongings. All was left behind—to be confiscated and sold at auction. Even Farshid's priceless Persian miniatures. His library of books. The family photo albums. Everything now belonged to the government of the United States.

Rose was outraged. It felt like a totalitarian police state!

Yet it was all perfectly legal under the USA Patriot Act, signed into law on October 26, 2001, by George W. Bush and quietly renewed under two subsequent administrations. According to the law, noncitizens could be deported without warning if suspected of promoting acts of terrorism.

Terrorism? "What are you talking about?" Rose felt her blood beginning to boil.

"Remember I told you that my father had been a part of the Iranian Revolution when he was a student in Tehran?" asked Bijan, trying to stay calm. He was referring to an event in 1979, when university students rose up to depose the Shah, a pro-American puppet who'd been installed as a monarch and was heavily armed by the CIA, which had also trained his brutal secret police force.

Rose remembered their conversation but was nonetheless confused. "Why'd they let you come here in the first place?"

"They didn't know," Bijan responded grimly. "Until now."

"But I thought the Muslim ban had been ruled unconstitutional." Rose was starting to hyperventilate.

"This has nothing to do with Trump," said Bijan.

Of the many Orwellian powers conferred upon the Department of Homeland Security by the USA Patriot Act was the blanket authority to conduct massive and indiscriminate surveillance of everyone within the United States—whether citizens or not—and even globally for that matter. This included web crawlers running twenty-four seven in massive server farms that analyzed social media activity—everything posted, browsed, and certainly anything liked.

They had sophisticated algorithms that used artificial intelligence to analyze actions and look for suspicious patterns. Certainly, a flag would have been raised if someone had posted the words "Capitalism" and "evil" in the same sentence, especially when accompanied by an exclamation point—that's what led them to Rose. Within nanoseconds of creating that post, she'd established her very own Homeland Security file on a server in Omaha. After Bijan hearted the post moments later, he had one, too—both of them created and managed by nine lines of highly classified computer code. The AI went to work, scrutinizing everything coming in and out of Rose's laptop.

She creates artwork that features revolutionary symbols. Interesting. She's reading a translation of a journal by her great-grandfather, who'd been arrested for revolutionary activities. Doubly interesting. Her father is a political consultant with a fondness for radical ideas. Let's give him a file, too.

Bijan, as an Iranian, received even more scrutiny. His parents, naturally, came under surveillance, too. The computer self-authorized its unfettered access to cross-check names against law enforcement databases, including Interpol records and watchlists held by the Israeli Mossad, which is where the algorithm detected a match with Farshid. Then, finally, a human was brought into the loop. Agent Toby Jones in the Culver City field office received a briefing memo, composed entirely by a computer, which caught his attention.

Even though Farshid Yadzani had only been peripherally involved in it, the Iranian Revolution remained an extremely sensitive matter within the Department of Homeland Security. If the war on terror had a beginning, it was then, when Iranian students captured fifty-two American hostages and detained them within the US embassy complex in Tehran, which they seized and managed to occupy for 444 days, dooming Jimmy Carter's hopes for reelection and ushering in the Reagan era.

Agent Jones brought the Yadzani case to his superior, who took one look at it and said: "Get that bastard out of our goddamn country."

CHAPTER 21

KISMET

I must have fallen asleep in the synagogue. I'd been bemoaning my predicament all night, praying, sobbing until the wee hours—beseeching a G-d I'd lost faith in long ago.

But that was all about to change.

For, next thing I knew, I opened my eyes to what can only be described as an angel. She was a woman in her forties, Magda Klein, diminutive and very pretty—the wife of the rabbi. She'd been watching me patiently, doing her needlework. Instead of berating me for sleeping in the sanctuary, she smiled sweetly and said, "Shalom."

She could tell I had been crying; my clothes were still damp from the rain.

I apologized for my disheveled appearance and for disrespecting the temple. But she just put a finger to her lips and whispered, "Ssshh," which reminded me of Comrade Rosa, whom I still missed, even after all these years.

"You must be hungry," said Mrs. Klein. "I'll bet you like brisket." My expression made her laugh. *Was I drooling?*

Moments later, I was wolfing down the most delicious brisket, latkes, and applesauce I'd ever tasted—a meal fit for a king!

Mrs. Klein kept giggling. "Slow down, child. You'll frighten the food!"

I couldn't help myself. After cleaning my plate so thoroughly that Mrs. Klein could easily have put it back in the cupboard, she asked me about my family, which caused my eyes to well up with tears. As I explained my sad situation to her, she took my hand.

Realizing I needed a place to stay, she mentioned her brother-in-law, Samuel Klein, the rabbi's younger sibling—he kept a spare bed for lodgers. "Can you do sums?" she asked. "He needs a bookkeeper for his carpentry business."

"I can build," I said, feeling suddenly more optimistic. "I'm a carpenter, too!"

"Let's go see him." She took my hand and led me up the rickety steps to the apartments in the attic above the temple, where all night I had prayed for solace. As I ascended the creaking staircase, I heard music floating down from above—the sound of a violin, coming from the apartment at the very top of the building.

Mrs. Klein rapped her knuckles on the door, and the music stopped, replaced by the pitter-patter of footsteps. A young girl of eight appeared at the doorway, fiddle in hand.

"My beautiful and very talented niece, Nadja," said Mrs. Klein with pride and affection. The girl was certainly endearing and, considering the sublime melody I'd heard through the closed door, a musical prodigy, no doubt—but what caught my attention and made me gasp was the object hanging on a silver chain around her neck. A white pearl with a clip-on clasp, whose distinctive shape I knew so well it could have been an extension of my own body. I literally could trace its contours with my tongue, since I had swallowed it so many times to hide it. My mother's earring!

A miracle? Absolutely!

From that day forward, I never doubted the power of prayer. We Jews call it kismet—akin to a trail of breadcrumbs sprinkled by G-d to lead you to your destiny. What was it that had compelled me to buy that sugared apple?

What had caused the seller to suggest a Nickelodeon at Union Square, fifteen blocks to the north? And what mysterious force had nudged the rain to come down precisely at the moment that I emerged from the theater, urging me to wander east and take refuge in this mysterious temple, where I was escorted upstairs to encounter this incredible child?

"You met my sister!" I exclaimed, producing the earring's twin, which Mrs. Klein regarded with fascination—proof that my family had made it to New York.

But as I did the math in my head, it made no sense. This girl hadn't even been born when my family had presumably arrived ten years prior. Besides, I had trouble reconciling that Sonya, under any circumstances, would have traded her earring away, given the pact we had made.

"I got this from Yael," said the girl.

"That's her cousin," Mrs. Klein explained.

Mrs. Klein, accompanied by Nadja and her violin, escorted me to the bakery on Delancey Street where Yael worked—all of us, excited to get to the bottom of what happened. Yael confirmed she'd offered the pearl as a gift to Nadja for playing violin at her wedding six months prior, but she, too, had never met my sister.

Yael had acquired the earring from Adolph Levy, whose son she tutored in Hebrew. Yael, as curious as the rest of us, tossed off her apron to join the quest and help solve the mystery of the parted earrings. We went from place to place in an ever-increasing group, one person leading to the next, with Nadja playing a jig on her fiddle like the Pied Piper as we moved through the streets of the Lower East Side.

Adolph Levy, a cobbler, had received the earring as payment for shoes from Gilda Heller, the librarian, who led us to the tailor, Morris Abrams, who explained that he'd been given the pearl by the Fishman family; they, in turn, had acquired it from Sarah Rickman, the stenographer. It went on and on. My mother's earring had been circulating through the neighborhood from person to person for ten years!

Finally—though it took the entire day—we came to the point of origin: an elderly, retired mason named Felix Steiner. Mr. Steiner was nearly blind and quite hard of hearing, but he vaguely recalled having received the pearl from a family just off the boat from Hamburg, in exchange for food and lodging.

"That's them!" I could hardly contain my excitement. Mr. Steiner couldn't specifically remember my sister, Sonya, but he certainly had a memory of Max.

"We talked about construction," said the former mason, squinting at the light from his window. "Your brother wanted to work on skyscrapers, so I said—Chicago."

"Chicago?" I was unfamiliar with it.

Mrs. Klein explained. A major financial, industrial, railroad, and trading hub, Chicago was in the midst of a building boom, which included some of the tallest buildings in America. I knew with certainty that's where Max would be.

After a week of getting my bearings and some much-needed rest, I boarded a train for Chicago. A handful of people from the neighborhood accompanied me to the impressive, newly-built Grand Central Terminal, including Mrs. Klein, Yael, Felix Steiner, and Nadja, who serenaded us with her fiddle, which reverberated gloriously as we crossed the cavernous lobby. The station was so large I was convinced that it could have contained the entire ship that I'd taken from Liverpool. The train I beheld on Platform 1 was equally extraordinary—a sleek, gleaming Pullman with eighteen luxury cars.

"That's the 20th Century Limited," said Mrs. Klein. "It goes ninety miles per hour!"

I couldn't begin to grasp it. Well-heeled passengers—porters and stacks of luggage in tow—strolled along a crimson carpet that ran the length of the platform.

"It's called the 'red-carpet treatment,'" she whispered. (Right here—on Grand Central Platform 1—is where that phrase originated.)

The train, apparently, had beds with linen sheets, a barbershop, secretarial service, gourmet dining, and plenty of booze. I was starting to see that, despite its reputation as an egalitarian haven, American society was just as stratified as the land I had left. Though the 20th Century Limited made a stop in Chicago, its fare exceeded what I had spent to cross the entire Atlantic—therefore, it was not the train I'd be taking.

Mrs. Klein had booked me, instead, on an ordinary train that departed from Platform 12. I waved gratefully to my New York friends, as Nadja continued to play her violin in honor of my departure. Then I turned to board the second-class car.

In Russia, all the rows faced forward on trains, but here the seats were arranged in benches that faced each other. I found a spot where—through kismet and camaraderie—I'd soon encounter another influential mentor and friend.

I noticed him immediately: a distinguished-looking gentleman in a three-piece suit.

He was puffing a pipe and gazing out the window as the train left the station. My first thought was: *Why isn't this man aboard the 20th Century Limited?*

After studying him for a moment, I pulled out the apple and biscuits that Mrs. Klein had kindly packed me for breakfast. I watched the man reach into his leather briefcase for a book that deepened the mystery—a translation of Maxim Gorky's *The Lower Depths*, a play I hadn't read but certainly had heard about. It was a brutal depiction of the lives of the working poor in tsarist Russia—so graphic that people had refused to sit in the first three rows when the play opened in Moscow around the time of my arrest. Gorky was also arrested for his writings, of course, which made him an even greater hero to the revolution. My fascination with this gentleman increased as he became intensely absorbed in this political play by a Russian revolutionary.

Then I pulled out a book of my own—*The Jungle* by Upton Sinclair, another gift from Mrs. Klein, who thought it would be a fitting introduction to Chicago, especially for a socialist like me. In the same vein as Gorky's play, *The Jungle* portrayed the harsh conditions and exploited lives of working-class immigrants, toiling long hours in Chicago's infamous stockyards. I'd begun reading it with great relish in New York, using my Russian-English dictionary to look up words I didn't know as a way to deepen my growing fluency.

Thus, laying the dictionary on the seat next to me, I opened Sinclair's scintillating novel to my bookmarked page and began reading where I'd left off, which was so fitting it made me smile:

One of the first consequences of the discovery of the union was that Jurgis became desirous of learning English. He wanted to know what was going on at the meetings, and to be able to take part in them, and so he began to look about him, and to try to pick up words...

Also the union made another great difference with him—it made him begin to pay attention to the country. It was the beginning of democracy with him.

As I went back and forth between my book and my dictionary, the gentleman seated across from me began to take notice. Increasingly intrigued, he soon put down his own book and watched me in fascination.

Finally, he couldn't help pointing out the irony: "You're from Russia! We should be trading books," he laughed. "Clarence Darrow." He extended his hand. "American socialist."

That's why he'd refused to travel on the 20th Century Limited.

"Joseph Rakow, Russian revolutionary," I responded, prompting other passengers in the car to look at us askance.

"My own ancestors fought in the American revolution to depose the British king, and look where we've come," he laughed. "A whole new class of royals in the court of Wall Street."

Bertrand Russell would have loved him!

In time, I'd come to know the impressive biography of the man who sat before me.

Mr. Darrow, a prominent civil rights and labor lawyer, had argued some of the preeminent cases of the time, such as the landmark Scopes "Monkey" Trial, where he'd defended the right of a school teacher to teach the theory of evolution in Tennessee. In addition to representing union activists and labor leaders, Darrow would also go on to become one of the founding members of the American Civil Liberties Union.

What so impressed me about this litigator was his curiosity and interest in the world and people around him. That's why he liked to travel in second class—to engage with "real" people like me. Indeed, Mr. Darrow could hardly contain his questions, especially after he learned that I'd been exiled to Siberia for revolutionary activities. He was intensely interested in my interactions with Russian magistrates and the system of justice under the tsar. "Injustice system," he joked, shaking his head sadly upon learning that defendants had no rights whatsoever at trial and no choice but to accept the brutal sentences that were handed down to them.

"Revolution is imminent," he declared. "Mark my words—your malevolent tsar will soon face a firing squad."

He was right. But it would take us another five years.

I don't remember falling asleep, per se—we'd talked late into the night. Feeling a nudge on my shoulder, I opened my eyes. The train had stopped. "We're here," said Mr. Darrow, stuffing a fresh wad of tobacco into his pipe.

"Welcome to Chicago!"

I felt a tinge of excitement, for I knew I was one step closer to the moment I'd been pining for. Mr. Darrow waited for me to gather my belongings, then we walked together onto the platform and across Chicago's train station, which, like the one we'd just left in New York, was also named Grand Central.

Emerging onto the street, I squinted into the bright sunlight. There were skyscrapers everywhere. Chicago seemed enormous, almost as big as New York.

Where would I even begin?

Chapter 22

So Close, So Far

FaceTime. What a curse!

Rose Simon never thought she'd feel this way. She and Bijan had used it countless times. Night, day, and any time in between. An instant way to conjure up the feeling of intimacy. It was like magic.

Her: "What in the world am I going to do about this hideous pimple?"

Him: "What pimple?"

Her: "Can't you see it? (Moving her iPhone into an extreme close-up.) It's so gross." Him: "All I see is that you're beautiful."

Her (blushing): "I wish you'd come over."

Him: "I wish I could, too." (Moving his iPhone to reveal the pile of study books on his desk.)

It could have been one of seven video calls they might have had on any given night, where living a few miles apart, they might have "technically" not been together, and yet, thanks to video-phone technology, they often were. Which brings us back to the strong emotions she was feeling during the summer of 2018, a few days after her chivalrous boyfriend from Iran (still awaiting a reply to his proposal of marriage) was suddenly and unceremoniously sent back to his country of origin—with no hope of returning to America anytime soon. What in the world was she expected to do about that?

They'd agreed to FaceTime at 10 a.m. for Rose in California, 9:30 p.m. for Bijan in Tehran. It was just moments away, and Rose began to freak out, with half a mind to call it off. Why torture themselves? The curse of FaceTime was that it would give them the illusion of proximity, even when they'd be eight thousand miles apart—almost halfway around the world. What was the point? What could they possibly say to each other?

Rose felt convinced her already broken heart might shatter into a million pieces. Plus there was the certainty that Homeland Security agents would be monitoring their conversation, which felt decidedly unromantic. Rose was beside herself, already in tears when the phone began to chirp.

She started blubbering the moment she saw his face. "I can't do this," she bawled.

Bijan tried his best to remain strong. "Sweet Rose," he whispered, wishing so desperately that he could wipe the tears trickling down those pretty cheeks.

This sucks, thought Joseph Simon, his adolescent heart aching for Eva Golden.

It had been like torture—their weekly meetings with Rabbi Weiss, where the two of them sat side by side on the settee, so close he could practically hear her heartbeat. Yet, Eva Golden remained entirely oblivious to his all-consuming infatuation for her.

"Just ask her to meet you at Menchie's," his buddy Eli had suggested.

As if it were that simple. Joseph wasn't looking to merely ask Eva out on a date. He was so smitten, he wanted to elope with her.

"So tell me, young scholars," began Rabbi Weiss, always chipper as he entered the study hall. "What have we learned about the human condition?"

"Wanna go first?" Eva turned to Joseph with a sweet smile. "I'm always hogging up our time."

Hog away, you amazing angel. That's the thought he had. What he actually muttered was "I'm good."

And off she went, in her melodic voice and enchanting mannerisms, talking up a storm about all the things she'd been thinking in that beautiful mind of hers. How Joseph wished that Eva could hear the thoughts in his head so he wouldn't have to speak them. How could he possibly communicate to her?

A poem. That's the way to do it. Like his great-grandfather had done for Comrade Rosa.

Who am I kidding? What do I know about poetry? Where would I even begin?

Joseph tried to channel his namesake ancestor. *What would Joseph have done?*

Start with the first line. You gotta start somewhere.

Joseph pictured his great-grandfather conjuring an image of his beloved Rose, which led him to visualizing a rose, prompting:

Roses are red...

He stopped himself immediately.

G-d, that's terrible!

It was hopeless.

"Not a chance, amigo," said Kyle Rotterdam, a Republican strategist, who'd just joined the reelection campaign of Congressman Ralph Trent as a communications expert.

"Gimme a break, Kyle," said John Simon, who knew him well. "We're polling in double digits."

"Not even close." Kyle held his ground. "My guy is kissing forty."

Classic bullshit, John thought. The latest *Chronicle* poll had Patti

Alvarado at 14 percent and Ralph Trent at 36 percent—hardly "kissing forty." It was still a twenty-point spread, however, and that's why Kyle Rotterdam was playing hardball.

John had gone head-to-head with him on half a dozen campaigns. Kyle was the guy the Republicans invariably called when one of John's longshots started to build momentum, which was beginning to happen with Patti Alvarado. That's why John thought the time was right for a debate.

With candidates so far apart on the issues, putting them on a stage together would invariably bring them closer in the polls—that's what a debate was designed to do: allow the public to compare. But debates were strictly voluntary, which is why Kyle Rotterdam refused to bite.

There was no upside for his candidate.

"Don't force me to play the 'chicken' card," threatened John. They both knew what that meant—a classic chess move in these types of races, where an underdog candidate like Patti takes to the airwaves, explaining that her opponent refuses to meet her on a stage.

"We'll have the debate without you," warned John into his speakerphone. "A townhall meeting where we face your Republican base. It'll show them that Patti's got balls, unlike your guy."

"She'll fall on her face," laughed Kyle. "She's a rank amateur."

"So what are you so worried about?" taunted John. "What's it gonna take?"

"She needs to get a heckuva lot closer."

"How much closer?" There was a pause.

"Her polling number needs to start with the same first digit as ours." *Ouch.*

That night Lani walked into John's office and sat for a moment, watching him work. "Ten weeks until Election Day," she said as John tried not to wince.

This conversation was bound to happen, sooner or later. It always did. Still, he'd been hoping for a little more leeway.

"We're closing in, honey," said John. "I can feel it."

Lani stared at him without saying a word—she didn't have to. They'd had this talk a million times. All of John's pro bono work had racked up some serious debt for the Simons. It wasn't just the longshot campaigns. Several years earlier—tired of slaving for all of these underdog candidates that he could never ultimately control—John had decided to run for office, himself, when a vacancy opened up in the California State Assembly. It was a disaster. On every possible level.

In a classic rookie mistake, John had decided to self-fund his campaign by taking a second mortgage on the house, which had put them in a very precarious position. The Simons might have been forced to declare bankruptcy were it not for Lani's high-paying job at the ad agency. And now that safety net was gone. With all of his experience in politics and relationships with elected officials, John could be making a lot of money as a lobbyist, which is what Lani had been urging him to do for years.

And that's what she was saying with her expression. The time to make that move was right now, while the jury was still out. If John were to suffer another defeat on Election Day, his stock would plummet. *Do it now*, she urged with her eyes.

They were close enough to communicate like this. Nonverbally.

I need more time, John responded telepathically. *Please.*

"I'm going to bed," she said and turned to leave. John sighed. So close—so far away.

CHAPTER 23

WINDY CITY

The bitter gusts ripping across Lake Michigan reminded me of Siberia. It was the kind of cold that seeped into your bones. My entire body felt like ice, especially my heart. I'd been in Chicago for three months—and still no sign of my family.

This place was colder than Russia.

Mr. Darrow, bless him, had a spare room above his woodshed, where he'd invited me to stay in exchange for handiwork around the house—of which there was plenty.

Rain gutters to clear of autumn leaves, cracks to seal as temperatures dropped, leaks to seal in the roof shingles. The home was pleasant, but slightly disheveled, like Mr. Darrow himself. He was not the most organized of fellows—piles everywhere, often losing things. He had a sense of humor about it, at least—joking that the only reliable file cabinet that he owned was the one between his ears. His intellect was sharp as a razor. Once a week, Mr. Darrow and his wife, Ruby, a journalist who was considerably younger than he, would invite me over for a meal and conversation. The rest of the time I was on my own.

I had one clue of my family's whereabouts: Chicago. And that had been told to me by a very old man. Was it reliable information? Who could know for sure? The only certainty I had was the need to keep my faith, no matter what. I knew all too well what could happen if I allowed doubt to enter my consciousness.

So, day after day, I did the one thing I knew to do—go from one building site to another in search of Max or my father. There were also yards across the city where immigrant workers with building skills would gather every morning in hopes of finding employment. I visited them in rotation each weekday, searching the myriad faces—forlorn, weathered, and lonely—from disparate nations: Irishmen, Italians, Hungarians, and Poles, many on their own like me. I befriended one such worker, Alberto Struppa, from Italy, who reminded me of my father. He was from the mountainous Abruzzo region, where he'd left his family behind—a wife and four kids—and was working hard to save money and send for them. In all his years of being here, Alberto was still only halfway to making his goal: two hundred dollars for five steerage tickets from Naples to New York.

Despite his experience as a builder, he could barely make a living wage.

While the Chicago construction boom afforded many jobs for those with skills, there was also a glut of workers. Several million immigrants were arriving every year to this place known as "the land of opportunity." On any given morning, half the laborers who showed up ready for work at the construction yards were left behind. It was "a buyer's market," Mr. Darrow explained—meaning buyers (the construction foreman, in this case) had the power to decide who to hire and what to pay, leaving the workers without recourse. While certain industries in Chicago, such as the garment trade, had begun to unionize, it was still every man for himself in the construction field—a grim situation Mr. Darrow wanted zealously to change.

Alberto, an old hand in the construction yards, taught me the tricks he'd developed over the years to maximize his chances of getting picked. Foremost among these was not to appear overly eager or desperate. He coached me to walk with quiet confidence toward the foreman's truck as it entered the yard, rather than running like most of the other workers, then signaling to him with a nod or a simple hand gesture to convey the impression, whether true or not, that we were already acquainted with each other. If the foreman believed he'd hired you before, he was more likely to do it again.

It took a little practice, but I was soon able to adopt the attitude that Alberto had suggested—and it worked! I found myself dragged unexpectedly onto a cramped truck with a dozen other workers and driven to a construction site, where they handed us each a sledge hammer and pointed to an enormous rock that seemed to be in the way of what they were poised to build. That was our assignment—demolish this boulder the size of an elephant. It was punishing work, fourteen hours of hard labor with no breaks and little regard for the toll this was taking on our bodies. We may as well have been inmates in a penal colony. And after all of that grueling misery, when every muscle ached and we could barely move, the foreman doled out our pay—two dollars.

The discussion in Mr. Darrow's dining room the following evening was impassioned, to say the least. He and Ruby were deeply upset about what I described, as was another guest that they had wanted me to meet—a young black man, about my age, by the name of Elijah Moses. Elijah worked in the hotel services industry, and Mr. Darrow was mentoring him to become a labor organizer. Workers across America urgently needed to be unionized, like workers everywhere. Mr. Darrow encouraged me to assist Elijah and learn from him. So I did.

It was similar to the work that Max and I had done in Pinsk—printing and distributing flyers to persuade workers to attend meetings. But it seemed far easier, ironically, to drum up interest in tsarist Russia, though workers there could be summarily executed for even attending these labor gatherings, which is why they were underground and clandestine. While labor meetings were perfectly legal here in the "Land of the Free," workers seemed far more skittish—particularly Chicago's hotel employees, who were almost uniformly black.

It may not have been demolishing boulders with a sledgehammer, but hotel work was just as harsh—with shifts running sixteen hours, sometimes longer. Service employment, moreover, required high concentration and constant focus. Nonetheless, these workers were very wary of unions. They didn't want to lose their jobs. Hotel owners routinely hired gangsters to intimidate workers from striking or joining unions. On more than one occasion, Elijah and I crossed paths with a pair of thugs who threatened to break our legs and would have succeeded, had we not managed to run away.

I became convinced that construction workers were also in dire need of a union. The movement needed a leader, too, and Mr. Darrow was certain that it should be me. While not entirely persuaded, I agreed to take the first steps and begin distributing leaflets with the help of Elijah.

Several days later, as we papered one of the construction yards with our flyers, never could I have predicted what was about to happen next. It began with a familiar voice, shouting: "Over here!" English, but with a Russian accent—so familiar to me. "Here!" I got chills.

It was Max!

I spun around, scanning the faces of the laborers vying to be chosen, calling out to the foreman. *Where was he?*

"Here!" I turned in the other direction and couldn't believe my eyes. Max wasn't amongst the workers but was standing on the truck—and wearing a three-piece suit!

"Skilled masons only," Max called out in his heavily accented English. "We are laying a foundation."

I couldn't believe it. Max was a foreman. He was the boss!

Workers were swarming him, desperate for employment, and Max was treating them like all bosses do—with thinly veiled disdain. I pushed my way forward.

"How about me?" I looked my brother in the eye, and his jaw dropped. We stared at each other speechlessly. Max looked like he was seeing a ghost.

"Me! Take me!" Workers shouted to get his attention. Max shooed them away and jumped down from the truck bed. He grabbed me in a fierce embrace.

"Oh Yosef, Yosef," he cried out in tears. "I thought we'd never see you again!"

Max turned suddenly and called out to the truck's driver: "Take over.

Six men. No complainers." Then Max escorted me out of the mayhem to the corner of the yard.

"Yosef, Yosef," he took me in greedily with his eyes. "You look good! So healthy."

I could have said the same thing about him. My brother turned and snapped his fingers to a nearby man in a uniform. "Bring the car!"

Max has a car? The surprises were just getting started, for it wasn't just any car—it was a Rolls Royce Silver Ghost!

"Bruno will take you to mother, I'll be there soon. I have a meeting with the mayor."

The mayor? My head was spinning.

Max gave me one last hug and darted off, as his chauffeur, Bruno, opened the car door. I stepped inside in wonder—it was the first automobile I'd set foot in, and probably the finest I'd ever experience. There were panels of inlaid wood, an upholstered seat, and silver flasks of whiskey. I was simply stunned. *This is Max's car?*

A whirlwind of thoughts swirled through my head as we crossed the city from the industrial flats to a residential neighborhood lined with trees. We came to a nice house at the end of the lane—bigger and better maintained than the one belonging to Mr. Darrow. Bruno jumped out to get the door.

"This is where we live?" I still couldn't quite believe it.

Bruno nodded. "Your mother's home."

I stepped out of the automobile and took it in. After a breath, I walked up to the porch. The door had a lion's head knocker with a ring in its mouth. I rapped it two times and waited. Footsteps approached; the door swung open.

My heart soared. But it was not my mother. I beheld a black woman in a maid's uniform. I blinked. *We have a maid?*

"Missus ain't here," she explained. "She's at the orphanage."

Orphanage? Was Mother adopting another child? Nothing was making any sense.

Although the orphanage was in walking distance, Bruno drove me and waited in the car. I entered the three-story brick building, both nervous and excited.

"I'm looking for Sophie Rakow," I addressed the receptionist.

"Third floor," she said. I climbed the steps in mounting anticipation and entered the large hall full of young children running around in excitement—an activity room, where they were making arts and crafts.

"Wanna see my violin?" one child approached me to show off the project he'd been working on—a small fiddle fashioned from a wood chip and bits of thread. I couldn't believe it. It was almost identical to the one I'd made as a boy in Russia!

That's when I saw her. My mother.

Surrounded by kids, Mother worked here as a volunteer, helping them with their art projects. She didn't notice me at first, until I came closer. Then Mother dropped what she was doing and rose to her feet in shock.

"Mother!" My eyes filled with tears.

Hers did too. "My kindela, my kindela!"

Mother shook her head in amazement at how much I'd grown and developed muscles from the hardships I'd endured. "Oh, Mother," I smiled. "I missed you more than you will ever know." She began to sob; she couldn't control herself. I pulled her close and hugged her with all my might. The orphans watched in fascination and bewilderment.

"This is my son," Mother blubbered through her tears. "My baby!"

Though I was hardly a baby, the orphans quickly understood what they were witnessing, and it moved them deeply, filling them with sudden hope. Here, before their eyes, was a child being reunited with his mother—the dream of every child in the room.

"My kindela, my kindela," Mother kept repeating, touching my hair with her slender fingers and looking deep within my eyes. "You're alive!"

I stared back at her—noticing her silver hair and a few additional wrinkles on her face. But those loving eyes—they had not changed one bit. "Oh, Mother, how I dreamt of this day!"

"My kindela, my kindela." She was beside herself.

Children all around us were welling up with tears, some of them openly weeping. "Hip hip hooray!" shouted the boy who had shown me his violin.

All at once, the other children joined in. "Hip hip hooray!" The entire hall burst into laughter and jubilation.

An hour later, we'd returned to Mother's house to have some lunch, which the maid was laying out for us. That's when the mood shifted again.

"Where's Sonya?" I asked. "Where's Father?"

Mother's face blanched. She looked at me in horror. "Oh Yosef, Yosef." She could hardly bear to tell me.

I was devastated to learn that Sonya had perished at sea. Her fragile lungs could not withstand the brutal conditions aboard their steamer. She had died like Mr. Kask and so many others on my ship. My heart felt like it was about to shatter. My poor sister. Beautiful Sonya. I would never see her again. They had buried her at sea.

I realized in that moment that Sonya, as I had suspected, was not the one who had broken the promise regarding Mother's earring. It was Max who had traded the pearl to the mason, Felix Steiner, in exchange for lodgings in New York.

I can only imagine the heartbreak that Mother had been forced to endure, losing her only daughter on the transatlantic crossing. Just like Mr. Kask's widow, she had no choice but to watch the body of her loved one plunge into the cold, dark waters and sink to the ocean floor.

"And Father?" I hesitated to ask.

He had made it to Chicago, but the journey had likewise taken a toll on his health.

He had died several years ago and was buried at Hebrew Benevolent Cemetery, which was a thirty-minute drive.

"Would you like to go see him?" Mother asked. I was quiet.

Then I said: "Let's wait for Max."

Mother explained that Max was unlikely to be showing up anytime soon. "Work, work, work. That's all he does anymore."

Bruno drove us to the cemetery, which sat on a grassy knoll not far from Lake Michigan. Mother escorted me to a headstone, and I stared at it with a heavy heart:

AVROM RAKOW
Beloved Husband, Beloved Father (1865–1908)

Cold, doleful winds whistled through the graves.

After paying my respects to my beloved father at the cemetery, I insisted that Bruno drive me to see Max. Mother had informed me, to my surprise, that she and Max did not live together—that Max had his own home in Forest Glen, an even more upscale part of the city.

As the Rolls Royce delivered me to what can only be described as a mansion, I tried to reconcile the brother that I'd known in Pinsk with this lifestyle that seemed so foreign to us. My first surprise came upon examining the nameplate at the front door. Not "Rakow," but:

Max & Bella Robin

Robin?

The next surprise was the butler who greeted me, a black man named Julius.

Butler?! (I suppose I should've been getting used to it by then.)

After I explained who I was, Julius invited me to take a seat in the parlor, which contained objects that I thought belonged only in museums—oil paintings, a suit of armor, a pair of canaries in an ornate cage, and a Victorian globe. Julius crossed to a cupboard where he extracted crystal glassware on a silver tray.

"Care for some whiskey, Mr. Joseph?" he asked. Having never tasted it, I declined.

"Cigar?" He opened a glossy box of inlaid wood.

I felt like I'd been transported to a different planet.

After lighting a fire in the hearth, Julius exited the parlor and left me sitting there with the crackling wood and ticking clock, which suddenly struck 8 p.m. in a cacophony of clamorous bells. Moments later, a beautiful woman, refined and elegantly dressed, entered the salon and introduced herself as Bella Robin, Max's wife. I admit to being slightly dazzled by her. She looked like one of the starlets of the Nickelodeon movie I had seen in Union Square. I explained who I was in English, and she seemed perplexed.

"I thought I'd met all of Max's family," she responded in Yiddish.

I was surprised to hear her speak Yiddish. She didn't even seem Jewish, although she was—but from Hungary, not Russia. Helping herself to a drink from the tray that Julius had left behind, Bella gazed into the fire and remembered that Max had spoken long ago about a younger brother—but she thought I had died.

"You're more muscular than Max," she said, looking me over. "How long will you be staying with us?"

I hadn't even begun to think about it. I felt dizzy from everything that had happened since that morning at dawn—which I realized was the last time I'd eaten anything.

"Would you like to bathe before dinner?" she continued in Yiddish. "And change your clothes?" Then she realized I hadn't brought a suitcase. I shrugged. Everything about this day seemed to be moving so fast. The grandfather clock struck half past eight—and that's when Max waltzed through the door, full of energy and enthusiasm.

"You've met my beautiful bride, I see," he said, giving me another big hug. Then Max clapped his hands. "Julius! Champagne," he commanded. "Our finest bottle. My brother is back—this calls for celebration."

Lighting himself a cigar, Max explained there was another reason to celebrate: he had just closed a deal with the mayor of Chicago to build another skyscraper.

"Remember how we used to play, building our mighty palaces as little boys?" He grinned at me. "Our dreams have come true, Yosef!" Max told me that I could be project manager of the new building, once I learned the ropes.

"Have you ever had a cocktail?" Max asked, as Julius popped open the champagne.

Of course not. I'd never even tasted champagne.

"This one's called a 'Prince of Wales,'" Max gleefully went to work at his bar. "Invented by the former king of England." He cut open a tropical fruit I had never seen (and later learned was a pineapple). Max squeezed its juice into a pitcher, along with "bitters" and "Maraschino liqueur," then he mixed in the champagne and stirred it up.

"Voilà!" He presented me with my first cocktail, pouring another for himself and one for Bella. "To your health," he said as he raised his glass.

I tasted the "Prince of Wales" and must admit I found it to be delicious. But I remained deeply troubled by what I was seeing in Max.

"Things are different in America," he said, as if reading my mind. "Anyone who works hard enough can live like a king. You redefine yourself."

"Is that why you changed your name?" I asked him pointedly.

"That was Bella's idea," grinned Max. "Don't you love it? She's a singer. A Robin. Get it?"

I was really struggling with all of these changes. "Why aren't you living in the same house as Mother? Why do you make her live alone?"

"Mother is not alone," he snapped. "She has a full-time maid!"

That was the final straw for me. I exploded in sudden rage and launched into a tirade against this brother that I hardly recognized. I couldn't believe that Max had turned his back on his proletarian roots—after all of our sacrifices. *My* sacrifices! I'd served ten years in exile for the cause, and now Max was behaving like the very people we'd been revolting against. I could tell that he was quietly seething as I concluded my diatribe, for he switched pointedly to English for his response.

"A lot has changed, Joseph." He looked me in the eyes. "You may have made some sacrifices. We all have. You have no idea what it was like to watch helplessly as the ship captain ordered his men to dump Sonya's body into the ocean."

Untrue. I had seen it with Mr. Kask—but I held my tongue.

"There's no sin in having money. In fact, it's a blessing. If we'd had money, our tickets would've been on the upper decks—and Sonya would still be with us."

I swallowed, seeing the truth in what he had spoken.

"I've worked like a slave to wrest this family out of poverty. If you choose to remain a pauper, so be it. I myself have no intention of changing my ways."

Chapter 24

Toldot

"I've got them in my own family," said Joseph in excitement, "a Jacob and an Esau!"

Rabbi Weiss, who had been hoping for Joseph to find a personal connection to the great fraternal rivalry depicted in the book of Genesis, smiled in delight. "Excellent, my young scholar. Tell us what you have discovered."

Joseph spent the next five minutes talking nonstop about the riveting story within the Rakow clan—describing the tensions between Great-Grandpa Joe, after whom he'd been named, and his Great-Grand-Uncle Max. Not only had young Joseph read the latest chapter of the memoir with relish and great attention, but he'd also done his own research this time, like his older sister, Juliette.

Overcoming impoverished roots in Russia, Great-Grand-Uncle Max had apparently built up a small empire in the United States, including several important buildings on the Chicago skyline, some of which were still standing. But he'd clearly paid a price for doing so, including tainting his relationship, it seemed, with his younger brother. But still—"You said *Toldot* means 'generations,' as in the things people generate with their lives." Joseph looked at his rabbi. "My Great-Grand-Uncle generated skyscrapers!"

"Indeed," said Rabbi Weiss. "But tell me—did this Great-Grand-Uncle Max have children?"

Joseph hesitated.

"Do you have any first cousins twice removed?" he asked the question in a different way. "Or is it second cousins, once removed? I can never remember."

"I'm not sure," Joseph admitted.

"Meanwhile, what happened with Great-Grandpa Joe?"

Joseph wasn't sure what was being asked of him, so the normally talkative Eva Golden jumped in and said: "He had kids, and they had kids, and one of those kids had you!" She was smiling right at him.

That's when Joseph realized something astonishing—for the first time (in forever!) he hadn't been obsessing about Eva. At least not for the last five minutes, anyway. Joseph had been all-consumed by something entirely different—his family tree and how that related to their Parsha.

He came into the room brimming with ideas and lots to talk about— even dominating their discussion this time, which is the role that Eva usually played.

"I'm so sorry." He looked at her and echoed her line from their last session: "I've been hogging our time."

"Hog away," she grinned. "It's fascinating!"

She thinks I'm fascinating. Wait—not me. She's talking about my family.

He was back in his head again. Caught in the web of obsessive thoughts.

"So, my young scholar," said Rabbi Weiss. "What are your conclusions?"

I gotta say something smart. What am I gonna say?

"Whose legacy will live on? Max's or Joseph's?"

Legacy? I'm so confused.

"Joseph's!" Eva jumped in. "Buildings eventually crumble, but a bloodline can go on and on."

Rabbi Weiss nodded in agreement. Then Eva turned to Joseph with a big grin. "But you'll need to have kids," she said. "Do you wanna have kids?" she asked, giggling.

Did Eva Golden really just ask me if I want to have kids?

"I dunno," mumbled Joseph, self-consciously. He felt like a piece of toast.

"I'll leave you with one last question," smiled Rabbi Weiss. "Of these two fascinating relatives, which is Jacob? And which is Esau? And, more important, which one are you?"

CHAPTER 25

REVOLUTION

"Pawn to Queen-Four," declared Mr. Darrow, puffing his pipe with gusto. He was blindfolded—so it was up to me to advance the white pawn for him, as he paced with deliberation toward the bookshelves that lined the back wall of his cluttered study. Mr. Darrow had been teaching me the game of chess, which I enjoyed immensely. Given his formidable mind and years of experience, however, he'd decided to handicap himself by playing without actually seeing the board.

"What's your response?" He turned in an abrupt about-face at the wall, knowing the confines of his workspace so well that he had no trouble pacing it blindfolded. I stared at the chess pieces. Mr. Darrow had explained the importance of controlling the board's center, so I decided to mirror his move: "Pawn to Queen-Four."

"Ah," he smiled. "Halting my advance."

Then, with two puffs and three paces, Mr. Darrow said: "Pawn to Queen's Bishop Four," which had me scratching my head, for he appeared to be offering up an unprotected pawn that I could easily take without repercussion. I checked the board carefully—nothing was guarding his second pawn. So I took it: "Pawn takes pawn."

Then he taught me the lesson: "Queen to Queen's Rook Four."

I slid his queen along the white diagonal and realized suddenly that...

"Check," said Mr. Darrow with obvious glee.

When I moved my white bishop to protect my king and simultaneously threaten his queen, which I felt pretty certain was a strong move, he was entirely ready for it: "Queen takes Pawn." I realized I'd fallen into a trap.

"It's called the Queen's Gambit," explained Mr. Darrow, removing his blindfold to refill his pipe and discuss the deceptive opening. "A metaphor for the ills of society, wouldn't you say, dear Joseph?" He smiled. "Sacrificing a lowly pawn for the glory of the queen."

I had grown fonder of my magnanimous host with each of these precious moments we had together. He enjoyed my company, too—because I often challenged him. "You told me to beware of deploying my queen too soon," I protested.

"Yes, the queen must be protected at all costs by her expendable underlings." He raised a mocking eyebrow. "But you also believe there's a time when our trusted leaders must actually lead us into battle, isn't that so?"

I realized that the discussion had transitioned suddenly from a chess lesson to a political debate. Conversations with Mr. Darrow were full of these pivots and surprises. That's what made them so enjoyable. He was alluding now to President Wilson, who'd been reticent to engage American servicemen in the bloody war raging across the Atlantic—a position that infuriated me, especially in light of recent events.

"They sank a civilian ship!" I exclaimed. "That could have been me on board."

Several weeks prior, on May 7, 1915, a German U-boat lurking in the waters near Ireland had fired a torpedo, which struck the starboard side of a 32,000-ton ocean liner en route from New York back to Liverpool. It was the RMS *Lusitania*, the very ship on which I had traveled!

The *Lusitania* had been crossing the Atlantic monthly since its launch in 1906— nearly one hundred crossings without incident, until that fateful day, which took the lives of more than 1,100 passengers, including 120 Americans. The German Embassy in Washington, DC, had issued a warning before the incident, cautioning Americans not to travel on British ships—a statement that was published in a New York newspaper in early May, appearing ominously on the same page as an advertisement for the *Lusitania*'s imminent departure from New York.

World War I had been raging for nearly a year, but America was not yet a participant; President Wilson had declared the United States would remain neutral, a position that most Americans supported. Britain, however, was one of America's closest trading partners—an alliance that Germany wanted to disrupt. After the attack, it was revealed that the *Lusitania* was carrying about 170 tons of war munitions for Britain, which the Germans cited as justification for their actions.

Mr. Darrow believed, however that, "They were simply goading us into becoming inextricably enmeshed in a costly quagmire that would only enrich the nefarious conglomerates that make weapons and warships, while pulling marionette strings to sway our political leaders." Darrow, like Professor Russell, was fundamentally a pacifist, as I was—believing that wars were waged by the elite, who used their influence and power to keep their own children off the battlefield, while spilling the blood of society's most disenfranchised. But this situation was different—at least that's how I felt.

"There's a moral imperative to act," I argued.

"Act? You mean to retaliate," he provoked.

"Killing innocent civilians is a crime against humanity," I asserted.

"And yet you're advocating for more killing." His litigation skills were far better than mine.

"Well, what does the Bible say about it?"

"An eye for an eye...," he responded.

"And you . . . subscribe to that?" I hesitated.

"Of course not! It'd make the whole world blind," he jumped in.

"The New Testament says, 'Turn the other cheek,'" I countered. "Is that what you advocate? They sink a civilian ship, we say: 'By all means, sink another.'"

"Touché, Joseph," he smiled, loving the fact that I'd used his own citation against him. It was like fencing. Strike, parry, strike. I could tell, in fact, that Mr. Darrow was less than convinced of the position he was arguing. He was merely enjoying a nice joust.

Indeed, when some months later, the Germans sank another ocean liner, the SS *Ancona*, this one from Italy, killing 270 people, including more than twenty-five Americans, Mr. Darrow came out publicly and vociferously in favor of mobilization in an impassioned speech.

"Pacifists are enemies of the Republic," declared the litigator to a crowd of Chicago laborers. "All those who oppose this war, who seek to confound our friends and hinder united action that alone can bring about victory, are working for the most despotic, arbitrary government that the world has known."

I nodded in satisfaction, wondering whether my views on the subject had played a small role in shaping Mr. Darrow's thinking. Public opinion in the United States had begun to turn against Germany, forcing Woodrow Wilson to change his position. By 1917, the president mobilized an army of five hundred thousand men to fight alongside their European brothers, which turned the tide of the war.

Meanwhile, in Russia, Joseph Stalin had been elected to the Bolshevik Central Committee, and Vladimir Lenin was leading a glorious revolution against the tyrannical reign of Tsar Nicholas, who'd failed the Russian people on all levels. His armed forces had been defeated badly on the field of battle; at home, there were huge shortages of food and people starved. The tsar tried to suppress the increasing riots, but he'd lost all credibility and was forced to abdicate his throne. By 1918, German forces had surrendered—and evil Tsar Nicholas, along with his family, had been executed. It was a great day for the proletariat. Workers everywhere rejoiced.

I took it as a sign to return to my role as an organizer of Chicago construction workers—an activity I had put on hold for a few years, since crossing paths with Max. I had not wanted to be at war with my own brother—but this mission was greater than both of us.

Chapter 26

The Issues

"Your opponent believes in 'Trickle-Down Economics.' How do you feel about that?"

"Well, how honest do you want me to be? You mean, trickling down on the heads of the working class?" Patti asked with a nervous chuckle.

Oh brother, thought John. *Thank G-d this is only a rehearsal.*

They were backstage on KZTV, Corpus Christi Channel 10—with Patti in a makeup chair, getting touch-ups in advance of an interview on the local prime time news. Landing this media slot had been something of a coup for John, who'd been scrambling for weeks to address the fact that Ralph Trent remained unwilling to participate in an actual debate with his candidate. John felt suddenly relieved about that—Patti clearly wasn't ready for a debate.

Clipboard in hand, Juliette at his side, John was grilling Patti on questions she might face, such as the one he'd just asked. "Trickle-down economics is the bogus and widely disabused theory that you can stimulate the economy by giving breaks to billionaires, who supposedly spend the money they save, thus spreading the wealth. But it's pure BS.

Billionaires never spend their money. They're notoriously cheap. That's how they become billionaires."

"I know," grinned Patti. "Just trying to lighten the mood."

John was glad she was feeling self-assured. He only wished he shared that confidence. He glanced at his list apprehensively. "Economics, education, immigration ... what else?"

"They might ask about gun control," chimed in Juliette.

"Don't get me started," said Patti.

"Careful," cautioned John. "I advise you to make your point and move on. The Second Amendment is an issue that entrenches the left and right in their respective positions. It gets very little traction in terms of poll numbers. Push it too hard, and you get accused of capitalizing on a tragedy."

"My daughter could've been killed, goddammit!" frowned Patti. "Don't tell me to move on." She was deadly serious—and full of fire.

Like a thoroughbred racehorse, thought John. *Loosen the reins and let her run.*

"Five minutes," said the stage manager through a crack in the door.

John went through his mental checklist. *What am I forgetting?*

"Closing remarks," said Juliette, explaining to Patti: "The anchor often gives you a chance to sum up the heart of your campaign."

"That has to be immigration," said John.

"But with a twist," added Juliette. Her father looked at her askance. Juliette realized she should have run her idea by him before blurting it to the client.

Loosen the reins, he thought. "Go ahead, Juliette."

She exhaled her idea in a single breath: "Tie immigration to the American Dream—like we did in our TV spot. Make the American Dream be about 'American Dreamers,' like longshot political candidates. Make it be about inclusion, about seizing back the narrative from patriarchal white men..."

"Two minutes," said the stage manager.

Patti looked at Juliette, then John. "She's good."

And off she went to the set, where she seemed entirely in her element, as if Juliette's remarks had been the perfect time-out pep talk. Sure enough, as predicted, the KZTV anchor gave Patti an opportunity to address the electorate directly. She made eye contact with the camera and said:

"I need *you* to help me use this election to prove that the American dream is for *all* of us, all classes and colors and genders of Americans—especially those among you hurting the most. Only with *your* vote can we show Ralph Trent and all the other naysayers that *anything* is possible in this great country of *ours*. He says the American Dream is for Americans. Well, I happen to be a proud Mexican-American. How about you? Are you fed up with politics as usual? Are you ready to help me stand up for—and reclaim—the American Dream?"

Wow, thought John.

Patti embraced Juliette as she came off the set full of exuberance: "The world needs more women like you. You're lucky. You were born in America. That means, unlike me, you can run for president. And you should one day."

Wow, thought Juliette.

CHAPTER 27

A ROSE BY ANOTHER NAME

The happiest and most important chapter of my life began in turmoil.

While the conflict in Europe—the bloodiest war in human history—was thankfully coming to an end, the loss of lives worldwide was to escalate even further, alas. And the killer, this time, was invisible.

They called it the "Spanish Flu." It appeared out of nowhere in the spring and summer of 1918 and spread like wildfire, at first amongst the massive numbers of troops concentrated in confined quarters. Soldiers coming home from Europe, packed by the thousands in transport ships, got sick in droves. Almost half of the US Navy contracted the deadly disease; and more servicemen died from the flu than had died on the gruesome battle-fields in Europe.

When the virus migrated from the military to the civilian population, the largest cities were the hardest hit. In Chicago, there had been a significant outbreak at the Great Lakes Naval Training Station. In the fall, Health Commissioner Robertson announced that officials had "the Spanish influenza situation well in hand now." But, of course, it wasn't.

A few weeks later, the city's hospitals were overflowing. Then Robertson declared: "Every victim of the disease is commanded to go to his home and stay there. No visitors are to be allowed." Pretty soon everyone knew someone who was sick or even dying. Then something started to spread that was even more contagious than the virus—fear.

Most wore kerchiefs or scarves to cover their faces. It was in the eyes that peeked out where I began to see distrust, anxiety, even terror of every man and woman I passed on the street. The invisible assassin could be anywhere. It spared no one. Even Max lost much of his bravado, as did Bella. Their wealth could not guarantee their safety—this killer did not play favorites, couldn't be bought off and sent away in a fancy car. So Max remained largely isolated within his mansion, leaving others to manage the construction of his skyscraper, which was beginning to hemorrhage money. Fewer and fewer workers were willing to show up at a job site, and those who did were demanding higher wages. Max blamed me, of course, though I had nothing to do with it. Fear can be as good an organizer as any man.

For my own part, I remained calm—and I owe this to my time in Siberia, which had taught me a great deal about the ups and downs of human emotions. The greatest of human frailties is the illusion that we are somehow in control. When one surrenders this, as I was forced to do during my exile, then life becomes so much more serene.

In Siberia, a star had come crashing down from space and very nearly could have spelled the end for Yosef Rakow. But this was not meant to be. In Chicago, a microscopic organism could likewise bring about my demise. The outcome in both cases was out of my hands. So what was the point of worrying?

My only concern was for Mother, as age is no friend to illness. But her attitude was like mine—if this was meant to be her time, so be it. Nevertheless, I ran her errands and brought her food and groceries, which were harder and harder to procure as panic grew. My best bet was to cross town before dawn and go to the market on Maxwell Street in the Near West Side neighborhood of Chicago—and this is where the Spanish Flu actually became the biggest blessing of my life.

A shoe came flying out of a doorway and hit me in the face! That's how I first encountered the woman who would become the love of my life...

I was walking down Maxwell Street when this leather missile came shooting from the doorway of a second-story balcony and thumped me on the nose. I looked up to see a young woman emerge with a sheepish expression. Our eyes met. It changed everything.

Massaging my sore face, I beheld an incredible, bold woman of unconventional beauty, gazing down at me—wielding the other shoe and a slightly sheepish expression.

"Sorry," she said.

A second figure came barging up to the railing—an indignant man, who glared at her. "Are you crazy?"

"I'll throw the other one if you don't apologize, you pathetic imbecile," she replied in defiance. They were speaking in Yiddish. Were they married?

Then another young man came out on the balcony, laughing and ribbing the first man. "That's what happens when you mess with Rose!"

Rose? I couldn't believe my ears. *Was that really her name?*

Burning with curiosity, I made a point of returning to Maxwell Street as often as I could over the next few weeks. I couldn't shake that image of her— eyes blazing, hair undone, shoe in hand, and cursing like a sailor. I kept gazing up at the window, but sadly no one appeared. The one-time encounter with this mysterious "Rose" had profoundly distracted me from my mission of braving the crowds on Maxwell Street in order to buy food for my mother.

Do I dare walk up the stairs and introduce myself? Too bold, I thought. But, then again, that's exactly what she was. Trying to build up the nerve to take the next step, I bought myself an apple from the pushcart across the street from her window. Upon lowering my facemask to take I bite, I heard a female voice: "Aren't you fasting?"

I spun around and there she was! Though her face was covered in a mask and I could only see her eyes, there was no doubt in my mind that this was the shoe launcher—this was Rose.

The last time I beheld those marvelous eyes they were twenty yards away. Now, at one-tenth that distance, they had me in a spell.

Fasting? I was confused.

"It's Yom Kippur," she explained.

I'd completely forgotten about the Day of Atonement, the holiest day of the year in Judaism, during which observant Jews are expected to fast, repent for our transgressions, and pray.

"I've fasted enough in my life," I said.

It piqued her curiosity, so I briefly described the ten years of hardship I'd endured in Siberian exile. "Come break the fast with us," she said, officially intrigued and lowering her mask. "We'll make up for some of those meals you lost in Siberia."

"And the quarantine...?" I queried.

"You're healthy," she looked me over. "I can tell. You survived Siberia." Rose, I would soon come to learn, was immensely practical.

That evening, having bathed and put on my finest clothes, I returned to meet her boisterous family—a dozen people sitting around a dining table, including Rose, her parents, eight brothers, an aunt, and an uncle. I entered timidly and no one turned. You had to be loud and aggressive to be noticed in a household like this. Rose put her fingers in her mouth and whistled like a locomotive to get everyone to shut up.

"This is Yosef Rakow," she announced. "He's from Pinsk."

A dozen set of eyes stared me down. There were two strikes against me. Not only was I a stranger to this household, but it was also a time of quarantine. Rose's father, Mr. Raff, set the tone by leaping up from his seat and welcoming me warmly. Having clearly been forewarned by Rose that I'd be joining them, he extended his hand without hesitation and escorted me to my place at the table. But her brothers glared at me with suspicion. *Who is this penniless greenhorn, fresh off the boat?* I could sense them thinking. As the second-eldest child and only daughter, Rose Raff practically ran the household, now that her mother was getting on in her years. She was indispensable. Even though it was inevitable that Rose would one day be leaving to start her own family, no one wanted that to happen anytime soon. So they interrogated me with nonstop questions. It felt like an inquisition.

When I started talking about the plight of workers in Russia and in America, they began rolling their eyes. While all of the brothers worked in various trades, they were vehemently antiunion. One of them, Reuben, though he was only sixteen, had connections to some union-busting mobsters, with whom I'd soon cross paths. The more her brothers attacked my views, the more Rose came to my defense. Her father, who could tell that I was an intellectual more than an observant Jew, was curious about how I'd learned to read English.

"I taught myself," I explained, which caught the attention of Rose's older brother, Phil, an electrician, surprisingly reserved and soft-spoken in this household of wild hyenas. Before I left that evening, Phil found a moment to pull me aside and give me something as a gift—a copy of Shakespeare's plays with a bookmark on *Romeo and Juliet*.

"You'll enjoy this," said Phil, a passionate reader himself. I was touched, especially after I dived into Shakespeare's story of forbidden love and came across: "A rose by any other name would smell as sweet..."

In Russia, her name had been Rosa. Here in America, I found myself more and more smitten by a fiery young woman named Rose.

And there was something slightly "forbidden" about our courtship. It wasn't simply that we were dating during a time of quarantine. It was also that Rose came from a household comprised largely of political conservatives, whilst I was a liberal to an extreme—a view that she shared, in defiance of her family, particularly when it came to women's rights. Women were still barred in America (and most of the world) from voting—a right they now enjoyed in Russia, following the revolution, and neighboring countries such as Lithuania, Latvia, and Estonia.

Rose was immensely practical and no-nonsense in everything that she did. She gave useful tips on how to present my case to workers—avoiding overly esoteric and philosophical arguments, in favor of simple facts. Men like her brothers were only interested in concrete ways to put more food on the table—as the one who brought the food to their table, Rose knew this all too well.

As cases of Spanish Flu began to subside in Chicago, workers were eager to get back to their jobs, and I was eager to ensure that they got the protections they deserved. Based on her sage advice, I changed the wording in my flyers. You may find this somewhat comical but, before meeting Rose, my pamphlets read as follows:

NOBLE WORKERS OF CHICAGO, PROLETARIANS UNITED WILL NEVER BE DEFEATED! JOIN WITH YOUR BRETHREN ACROSS THE GLOBE!

After my conversations with Rose, the wording became:

DO YOU WANT SHORTER HOURS AND HIGHER WAGES? COME LEARN WHAT A UNION CAN DO FOR YOU!

It made an immediate difference. Suddenly, there were a dozen laborers at my evening meetings, sometimes more. Laborers had, by and large, stopped wearing masks by now and began to talk about the idea of organizing with great gusto. Momentum started to build. A measure of my success came in the form of increased harassment by antiunion mobsters. One evening after the meeting I found myself confronted by two goons named as only goons can be—a giant they called "Shorty" and a three-hundred-pound gorilla nicknamed "Feather." They told me that continuing to do what I was doing could be injurious to my health.

"And stay away from Rose Raff while you're at it," snarled Shorty.

I knew immediately who was behind this—Rose's teenage brother, Reuben, who, despite his young age, ran a numbers game for the Chicago mob and was one of the most vocal and protective of Rose's brothers. He had apparently enlisted these thugs to scare me.

Feather pulled a silver dollar from his pocket and "magnanimously" offered me the option of taking the coin in exchange for their mercy, thereby avoiding a beating. I realized this was a different kind of test—a test of my valor. Having had plenty of experience confronting men like these in the Russian penal system, I declined the coin to their bewilderment and amusement. They came after me, but because they were too tall and too fat, I had a decided advantage. I used my stealth and speed to run circles around them, landing excruciating blows to their kidneys, which had them howling in pain. A kick in the shin made Shorty bowl over, and then came my upper-cut, which sent him to the ground. I used a similar tactic to dispense with his partner.

The following morning, as I walked down Maxwell Street toward the Raff residence, I noticed Reuben in the alley playing dice with some of the neighborhood boys. I tapped him on the shoulder and flipped him the silver dollar, saying: "I think this belongs to you."

He had, of course, heard of my altercation with his thug friends—and, by the look on his face, I could tell I'd won his begrudging respect.

One of many things that drew me to Rose was her hands. They were con-stantly in motion, like birds in flight—grasping things, fixing things, keep-ing her unruly brothers in check. She spoke with her hands, like my Italian friend, Alberto—and, more important, as Rose would say from time to time: "I think with my hands."

As a carpenter, I knew exactly what she meant. Whenever I needed to clear some mental space for contemplation, often the best way to do so was to begin a simple manual task like whittling a piece of wood. By engaging the body in a fairly menial chore, my mind would then be free to expand into the realm of imagination.

I could see that happening with Rose, as she cooked for the family or did some sewing. I loved to watch her when she was busy and lost in her own world. The more time I spent with Rose, the more fascinated I became with those marvelous hands. I started to imagine what it would be like to hold them.

I remember one morning in early June 1919; I passed a newsboy who was shouting out "Extra! Extra! Congress passes the Nineteenth Amendment!" I snatched a paper out of his hands and went racing in a full sprint to Maxwell Street. Bolting up the steps to the Raff apartment, I was completely out of breath when Rose greeted me at the door.

"You can finally vote!" I grinned, holding up the newspaper in elation. "How do you feel?"

Rose nodded in satisfaction, then took the paper out of my hands to touch the headline physically. She wanted to savor the moment, to literally feel it.

"I 'feel' with my fingers," she smiled.

Things were changing rapidly in American society. Besides enacting universal suffrage, the states had also ratified another amendment to the Constitution, banning the sale and distribution of alcoholic beverages. This had little effect on my own life but was devastating to Max and Bella, who could no longer indulge in their penchant for champagne—at least, not legally. Speakeasies sprung up like mushrooms in the back alleys of Chicago. Bella began wearing boas and jeweled headbands and cut her hair in a wavy bob in the manner of flappers. She was, apparently, excellent at the latest dance craze—the "Charleston"—though I never saw it with my own eyes. This was not my world—though, later that year, with the Spanish Flu largely gone, I did have the experience of attending my first wedding.

It was the marriage of Rose's cousin, Sarah Raff, to Adam Cantor, who, befitting his name, was the cantor at their temple. Needless to say, there would be no Charleston at this orthodox affair. In fact, men and women were separated on opposite sides of the aisle. Throughout the ceremony, I stole glances at Rose as the couple took their place under the chuppa. I found myself deeply moved, imagining how this moment must have felt for my parents and for couples going back to Biblical times—an unchanged tradition, binding a man and a woman. When I glanced over at Rose, she was staring back at me, then she looked away modestly. Did she blush? No—Rose was not a blusher. I was projecting. If anything, it was me who may have blushed. My feelings for Rose, I realized, had begun to take on a life of their own.

Though we were in separate lines when the dancing began, I couldn't take my eyes off of her, watching Rose laugh and spin with her cousin Sarah.

When it came time for the Horah, Rose pushed her way into the circle, to the horror of the rabbi, and joined her brothers in lifting Sarah up in her chair. No one could have stopped Rose from being a part of that. As the giddy couple held onto their uplifted chairs for dear life, the band began "Hava Nagila." Rose winked mischievously as she paraded past me, carrying her cousin's chair—but then she lost her footing suddenly and almost went sprawling. I lurched forward with my hand. She grabbed it.

A bolt of electricity shot up my arm and into my heart. It was for the shortest instant, before disapproving stares from the rabbi and others forced us to part ways. But I will never forget that moment. We had held hands!

After months of courtship, the time had come to introduce Rose Raff to my mother. We chose a Sunday—Mother's day off from her volunteering duties. Rose brought a loaf of challah and a kugel she had baked, even though it was not a holiday.

But as we approached the house, I was surprised to see Max's Rolls Royce parked outside, with his chauffeur, Bruno, playing solitaire in the front seat.

Max and I had been avoiding each other for the most part, except for special occasions like the High Holy Days, where we'd maintain a cordial but reserved relationship. I was disappointed that he'd happened to have chosen to visit Mother on the very day I was bringing Rose. I had half a mind to call it off, but Rose told me it would be fine—she could handle anything.

When we entered, Max, surprisingly, was not there. Instead, we came upon Bella and Mother having tea in the dining room. There were expensive-looking cakes and fruit tarts that Bella had brought, along with flowers—luxuries that were extremely difficult to procure in these challenging times. I knew at once what Bella was up to—currying favor with Mother in hopes of persuading her to influence me to curtail my unionizing of the Chicago construction workers, which by then was affecting Max.

Mother lit up upon meeting Rose. She'd heard about her, of course—and there was an immediate warmth between them, which made me so happy.

Then Bella, in her long pearls and short dress, sidled up to Rose and said, "You're so lucky to have a man like Yosef ... So handsome, so strong." Bella gazed at me, flashing a shamelessly alluring lipsticked smile, which Rose saw right through.

"Luck has nothing to do with it," she retorted. "We're getting married."

My jaw dropped. For weeks now I'd been mustering up the courage to propose—but we'd just never discussed it until that very moment. Rose, in her take-charge manner, had beaten me to the punch.

Mother was ecstatic. "Congratulations, Yosef!" She gave me a warm embrace and then went to hug Rose. "I'm so happy for you two!"

"Yes," agreed Bella. "We should have a party."

But when Bella moved to embrace me, Rose gave her a look that stopped Bella in her tracks.

Two days later, the persuasion campaign continued—not Bella this time, but Max, himself. Rose and I were about to sit down for a quiet meal together that she had taken great pains to cook for us. Since we were under my mother's roof, we were taking advantage of the fact that she was out at the orphanage that evening—to have our own private celebration, just the two of us!

Suddenly, there was a loud knock at the door. It was Max, his chauffeur in tow, carrying a basket of goodies.

"I heard your fantastic news, little brother," said Max, slipping a chilled bottle of champagne from Bruno's basket. "Smuggled in from France! My bootleggers have performed miracles. Let's celebrate!" He hadn't even said a word to Rose, which made her immediately distrust him.

"Remember that cocktail you loved—the 'Prince of Wales'?"

"There are no 'princes' here," Rose said pointedly. Max continued nonetheless to concoct his cocktail, which he distributed to both of us.

"To our health, our wealth, and to our success," he said, raising his glass. Then, on the subject of 'success,' it didn't take long for Max to raise the real reason for his visit— to complain about overruns on the skyscraper, which were costing him a fortune.

"Why don't you sell your Rolls Royce?" I suggested.

Max exploded, calling me "self-righteous," along with other names I'd rather not repeat. I shouted back at him, and it quickly escalated into an all-out fight. He claimed that unions were "un-American," and that my activities could ruin the family fortune. I told him that his activities were ruining the family's soul. We were about to come to blows—Rose broke it up with her siren whistle, so loud it could stop a stampede of bulls. It was quite effective for fights between brothers, of which she'd seen her share. She told us to stop this ridiculous arguing and, always the pragmatist, instructed us to sit down and eat the dinner that was already on the table.

After doling out bowls of her delicious goulash, which we ate in silence for a moment, Rose made a comment about how all males were "cavemen"—now that women had the right to vote, we'd soon have a woman president, which would mean we wouldn't have wars and people wouldn't be starving. Max smirked at what he thought was an absurd fantasy. He still had very conservative feelings about the suffragette movement. Rose was able to take that in stride—but what caused her to finally hit the roof was when Max suggested callously that he take us out to celebrate properly with a "real" meal at the Walnut Room, one of the few upscale clubs in Chicago that allowed women diners.

That's when Rose threw him out of the house—Max couldn't believe how she literally pushed him down the hallway and slammed the door on him. Then we finally had the meal we had planned for just the two of us.

One month later, we were wed at City Hall—with Clarence Darrow as our witness, Alberto as my best man, and my fellow union organizer and friend, Elijah, as my groomsman, along with Rose's brother, Phil, the one who had given me *Romeo and Juliet*. And of course, my beloved mother.

Max was conspicuously absent, along with Bella.

Weighing even heavier than the missing Max was the fact that Sonya and Father were no longer with us. I'd always be a son and a brother; I could now call myself a married man. Mother wept—I was no longer her baby.

Chapter 28

Vows

"Is that when Great-Grandpa Joe became a US citizen?" asked Samuel, the youngest, at the family dinner table. "The moment he married Great-Grandma Rose?"

John nodded——he was making an assumption that the system worked like the present day. Rose Raff had been born in America, which meant she had full citizenship. Therefore, just as when Patti had married Enrique and became a citizen, so, too, should that have applied to Joseph Rakow.

But Juliette, increasingly steeped in her investigative research of the period, had a hunch it might not be that simple. "Don't forget how the deck was stacked against women back then." Keeping her phone below the table in the hopes that no one would notice, she did a quick search and came up with something alarming:

"I knew it!" she exclaimed. "Great-Grandma Rose actually lost her citizenship when she married Great-Grandpa Joe."

"*What?*" Rose couldn't believe it.

Juliette read the information off her screen: "The Expatriation Act of

1907 decreed that US women who married noncitizens were no longer Americans!"

"A law passed by men, of course!" Rose shook her head.

Lani was outraged—and sufficiently intrigued to forgive the presence of the phone at dinner. "What's the reasoning behind that law?" Lani asked her husband incredulously.

"Beats me," John said. "Same reason we create barriers for immigrants today, I guess."

Little Joseph wanted to get it straight: "So you're saying that when Rose said, 'I do,' she actually lost her citizenship?"

"Yup," said Juliette. "And get this—if the roles had been reversed, it would not have been an issue. If the man had been the citizen marrying a newly arrived woman, she'd get to piggyback on his citizenship without a hitch."

"What a double standard!" gasped Rose.

Samuel was thoroughly confused. "So neither of them were citizens?"

"They must have gone through the naturalization process," said John, "which probably meant three years of residency..."

"And—renouncing all allegiance and fidelity to any foreign prince, potentate, state, or sovereignty," Juliette read from the government website, "particularly the ruler of the country where the applicant first came from."

Rose laughed. "I doubt Joseph had any trouble renouncing his allegiance to the tsar."

Juliette explained that they also had to pass a test, answering basic questions about the Constitution, where exam administrators might ask: "If you were employed at a certain place and went on a strike, would you obey the instructions given you by your union before obeying the law or the mayor of the city?"

John shook his head. *Wow.* "The government was already wary of the labor movement—probably a result of so many immigrants with socialist views..."

That's when Juliette looked down at her phone in horror. "Dad! We've got a problem!"

She shoved the screen in his face. He blanched and then turned to his wife with a look that did not require words. Lani sighed as John and Juliette abruptly left the table. This was exactly why she didn't allow devices at dinner. She was upset, also, by the fact that Juliette had decided to take a semester off from Amherst to work on the final stretch of this dark-horse candidacy, which was becoming all-consuming for both of them. Every campaign seemed to have a crisis right before Election Day—and this particular time there was an added wrinkle: Joseph's bar mitzvah was in two days.

Dear G-d, help John to do the right thing, she prayed.

Patti Alvarado was not legally eligible to run for Congress and should therefore be disqualified from the race—that was the premise of a lawsuit filed in Federal Court by the Ralph Trent campaign. It was a variation of the "birther" argument leveled against Barack Obama in 2008 with a twist that involved Patti's wedding to Enrique that same year, which the lawsuit claimed was invalid—which meant, according to Congressman Trent, that Patti Alvarado was not, in fact, a citizen.

John wanted to be informed before calling the Alvarados. "We gotta see the exact wording of their filing," he said.

Juliette was already on it. She signed up for the "Free Trial" at Thomson Reuters, which gave her instant access to all publicly filed court documents. Scanning the complaint, she briefed her father on the essence of their argument: unlike when running for president, you don't need to have been born in America in order to serve in Congress—you are required, however, to have been a US citizen for seven years.

John knew from the political TV spot they'd recently cut that Patti had taken her citizenship oath on January 2, 2012. This was 2018—not seven, but six years later. "Oh shit," he said in sudden panic. But he was missing the point.

"That's not the issue, Dad," said Juliette. "The law says seven years to serve in Congress, meaning by the time she's sworn in, which would be January 2, 2019." Seven years, exactly.

The Trent lawsuit was claiming, however, that Patti had no right to take the citizen oath in 2012 because she hadn't met the criterion to do so—namely, being legally married to a US citizen for a period of three years.

"But the Alvarados were married in 2008," said John.

This is where the politics got ugly. The Trent campaign had hired a private detective agency to look into the matter. They were contesting the validity of that marriage, saying that the couple was living apart for much of that time or in separate bedrooms. Enrique was having affairs with other women. In other words, the marriage was a sham, and therefore the citizenship date was invalid.

John stared at Juliette in speechless shock. *Could any of this be true?*

CHAPTER 29

THE FALL

Things were getting increasingly tense between me and Max. In his efforts to finish his building, he'd been pushing his workers to their limits, and people were getting hurt. One carpenter from Poland, Lech Patarski, had lost a finger when a saw slipped.

They hadn't bothered to send him to the hospital; the foreman had bandaged him up on site. Even more outrageous—they forced him to finish his shift! It made my blood boil.

Lech and some other workers came to me in secret and said they wanted to form a union, so I convened a meeting. My best man, Alberto, was also working for Max at the time, and I was hoping that he would show up. But he didn't.

Afterward, I went to call on Alberto at the tiny basement studio where he lived. Clearly nervous to see me, he glanced left and right in the alley before admitting me into his modest room. "They've been following us," he whispered.

Alberto explained that workers at Max's site were being harassed by mobsters, warning them to steer clear of union organizers like myself. Alberto could get into big trouble if they found out that he was talking to me.

"I want to finish this job without complaining," said Alberto, explaining that he was one month shy of saving enough money to send for his family. "I haven't seen them in six years," he sighed wistfully, showing me a faded photograph of his wife and four small children, who were all grown by now. Would they even recognize him? Would they know who he was?

"Of course!" I assured him. Children are connected to their father for life. Long separations cannot erode that. He was comforted by my words, but I found myself suddenly emotional—seeing the parallels in our stories. I missed my father, my "Tate," more than ever.

I understood completely where Alberto was coming from—he just wanted to keep his head down and finish this last job, which would give him sufficient savings finally to buy five third-class tickets from Naples to New York. I couldn't wait to meet his family. The last thing I wanted was to get Alberto into trouble. So I bid him farewell and wished him the best. That was the last time we ever saw each other.

Two weeks later, a terrible tragedy occurred. This is how it was described to me by workers who witnessed it: Alberto had been working a double-shift and was exhausted, when Max's foreman sent him to the top floor of the skyscraper to retrieve the welding equipment they'd left out on the girders. The elevator was out of order, so Alberto had to climb sixteen flights of stairs. It had begun to rain, and the steel I-beams were slippery. As he bent, out of breath, to lift up the bulky acetylene canisters, Alberto's foot slid out from under him. He couldn't hold on.

With a desperate wail I cannot even begin to imagine, Alberto fell 160 feet to the ground and died instantly. My heart shattered when I heard the news, as if I had taken the fall myself.

Noble Alberto—how hard he had worked, and for what? I was beside myself, thinking about the poor family, who would never see their father again.

A few days later, I took it upon myself to arrange for his funeral at the Holy Family Catholic Church in Little Italy. The casket had to remain closed—so disfigured was Alberto from the cataclysmic fall. As the priest began the service, I looked around and was disappointed to see that, other than Lech Patarski, none of Alberto's coworkers were present. The place was practically empty.

Outraged, I went outside and discovered the reason behind this. There was a Model-T parked across the street, with two men watching people coming in and out of the church—my old friends, Feather and Shorty. I stormed over to them in a fury.

"How dare you?" I shouted. "Disrespecting the dead!"

"Just doing our jobs," said Shorty, lighting himself a cigarette.

"Take me to see him," I demanded.

"See who?" snickered Feather.

"*Who?*" I was practically apoplectic. "Your boss! My brother!"

I grabbed the tire iron affixed to the side of their car and began to smash the headlights. "*Whoa!*" shouted Feather, trying to calm me down. "Okay, okay!"

They knew from our last encounter I was not someone to be messed with, so they drove me to Max's office, which was on the penthouse floor of a twelve-story skyscraper on South Dearborn Street. When Max's secretary told me he was busy, I raised the tire iron I was still carrying in no uncertain terms, and she quickly summoned Max, who emerged, all smiles, from the double doors of his office.

"Yosef! So good to see you."

"You're coming with me."

"I wish I could. My schedule..."

"Now!"

I wielded the tire iron. Max could tell I meant business and hastily decided to follow me. We rode down the Otis elevator in silence. Once at the curb, I ordered Shorty to drive us back to the church, where the service had just concluded. The priest was inviting mourners—just Lech Patarski, at this point—to pay their respects. I forced my brother to approach the casket, which I opened.

"Look at him," I growled. My brother winced and had to turn away.

Alberto's contusions from his sixteen-story fall were so severe, he barely looked human. His face had been flattened grotesquely; his arm twisted at an unholy angle. I was so irate and disgusted I could hardly speak.

"He was a father," I hissed, "like Tate! He had children... he had dreams!"

I spun toward Lech, who was waiting for his turn to say good-bye to Alberto. "This man lost a finger on your job site!"

In my brother's silence, I could tell the reality was hitting him.

"Where is your heart? Where is your *humanity*?!" I continued my tirade. "You're a monster! I don't even know you anymore..."

That's when my brother broke down, embracing me in tears and whispering: "Forgive me, forgive me."

In the weeks that followed, Max finally agreed to unionize his construction workers, providing safety measures, reasonable hours, and bonus pay for overtime work. The irony of it was that, in doing so, Chicago's most skilled and talented craftsmen suddenly flocked to Max's job site.

The "Mighty Palace" was completed on time—and under budget.

Chapter 30

Taking a Stand

What began as a fall … became a fall from Grace.

"It happens to the best of us." That's how Patti Alvarado began her press conference to respond to the lawsuit filed by her opponent, Ralph Trent, in which he was attempting to have her disqualified from the race. Her prepared statement was remarkable in its candor, laying it all out in graphic detail.

The fall happened in 2009, less than a year into Patti and Enrique's marriage. He was atop the roof of a three-story mansion he'd been contracted to remodel. A pair of pliers slipped out of his grip as he worked to remove the flashing around an air vent. The tool slid into the gutter. When Enrique went to retrieve it, the roof joist he was standing on gave way—the eaves had been infested with termites and dry rot. He went tumbling to the ground. It could have been curtains.

Enrique used his arm to break the thirty-foot fall. His wrist got shattered and so did his right hip.

He needed several steel rods and months of rehab. Enrique had bid the job as an independent contractor, so the homeowner was not an "employer" and therefore not required to carry workers' compensation coverage; nor did Enrique have his own disability insurance, which was quite costly in the construction trade. So he was sidelined, unable to provide for his new family, while medical bills piled up.

Due to the excruciating nature of his pain, the surgeon prescribed Dilaudid, which proved to be a problem—Enrique quickly built up a tolerance to the opioid, requiring more and more. He began secretly crushing the pills and snorting them for faster relief. The secrecy and increasing dependence added to his feelings of shame, pulling Enrique into a downward spiral.

He found a street source for oxycodone, and before long—he was an addict.

Patti told him to get his act together, but it was too late. The addiction was controlling him. He began acting out in other ways with alcohol and other substances, blacking out with regularity, and acting impulsively and irrationally. He'd become an entirely different man from the one she'd married.

Patti was deeply disturbed. In her feelings of panic and helplessness, she moved out with Alexa into a church shelter for women in need. Things got worse before getting better. In his loneliness, altered consciousness, and increased isolation, Enrique sought the company of other women.

"Yes, our marriage was in serious trouble," Patti told the assembled reporters, who were practically salivating. "But we fought to save it. And our relationship is now stronger than ever."

When Patti enlisted Enrique's family to stage an intervention in late 2011, he came to his senses and entered a rehab program in Mexico, where he was able to clean up and begin on the path to recovery. His sobriety date was the same date that Patti took her citizenship oath. Enrique hadn't touched drugs or alcohol in nearly seven years.

"We beat this disease that's been devastating families all across the state by doing the one thing that can save you—sticking together through thick and thin."

With that, surrounded by Alexa, Enrique, and his entire family, Patti concluded her prepared remarks and fielded questions from reporters. The first one was about John.

"I noticed your media advisor is not present," asked the reporter from KRIS-TV. "Has he abandoned your campaign?"

"Hardly," said Patti. "John is where he should be—with his family. It's a very important weekend for them. His son is becoming a man."

John was brimming with pride as he led his family into the Valley Beth Shalom synagogue in Encino, where they'd shortly be partaking in a ritual that went back to Biblical times: the bar mitzvah of his son Joseph. The Simons looked sharp: girls in elegant dresses, boys in suits and ties.

"You got this, kiddo," said John, putting an arm around Joseph. "We're so proud of you."

"Thanks, Dad," said Joseph. He was proud of himself—of what he was about to say. It had all come together in the last few days.

"Phones off," Lani looked pointedly at John and Juliette. "Not vibrate. Off."

"Didn't even bring it," said Juliette. "It's in the car."

"Ditto," John chimed in. He, too, was proud of himself.

Even more surprising, neither he nor Juliette had even watched Patti's press conference earlier that morning. After some self-reflection, John had come to realize that there was nothing he could really do at this point for Patti Alvarado. It was in the hands of the electorate now. Candidates and campaigns would come and go. There'd be wins and losses. But the bar mitzvah of his eldest son—that happened once in a lifetime. And he intended to be fully present.

"You good, Samuel?" He took the hand of his youngest son. "This'll be you, in two years."

"Stop freaking me out, Dad," Samuel squirmed out of his grip.

"Just a heads-up that I am bringing my device," mentioned Rose to her mother. "Hope you're okay with it."

"Hello, Mrs. Simon," said a figure on the screen. It was Bijan,

FaceTiming from Tehran, where it was 10 p.m. "I didn't want to miss this."

How sweet, thought Lani. Rose was beaming.

Rabbi Weiss greeted the Simons as they entered the temple. They exchanged pleasantries with the family of Eva Golden.

"Good luck." Eva squeezed Joseph's hand.

"You, too," he whispered back. She looked so pretty in her lace dress, which he was able to admire now without going into a spiral of giddiness and confusion. *Is this what it means to be a man?*

His feelings for Eva had developed, over their months together, into something more complex and interesting than that initial zap by Cupid's arrow, which had kept him paralyzed and tongue-tied. In a surprising turn, Joseph had come to see Eva as an actual human being, rather than a mythologized creature. And, best of all, he liked her. They'd become friends.

"Let's do this," she grinned, as their two families took seats in the front rows of the sanctuary.

Lani kept an eye on John as the ceremony got underway. Seeing his lower lip starting to quiver almost immediately, she discreetly prepped a box of tissues that certainly would be required. John almost lost it when his mother, Saralie, and father, William, approached the Bimah for the first Aliyah, where close relatives of the boy being honored take turns reciting portions of the Torah in Hebrew.

When it came time for Joseph's parents and siblings to chant an Aliyah, John blubbered his way through it, giggling nervously in order not to weep.

Then came the moment they'd been waiting for, when Joseph stood alone at the Bimah as a matriculated member of the congregation—a "son of the commandment," meaning fully accountable for his actions in the eyes of those who subscribe to the Jewish faith. As such, Joseph would now give his interpretation of this week's Torah portion.

May my voice not crack, prayed the thirteen-year-old as he cleared his throat and unfurled his notes. Joseph's job was to find the personal and contemporary relevance of *Toldot* (Genesis 25:19–28:9), which tells the story of strife within a Biblical family of yore. After twenty childless years, Isaac and Rebekah finally conceive, but the pregnancy proves difficult with twin boys literally fighting in the womb and continuing that rivalry throughout their lives—a drama that plays itself out in every family, and even between nations. While Esau was a carnal man, Jacob was the spiritual one, yet he used deception to trick his brother out of his birthright and get the blessings of his father—a ruse in which Rebekah was complicit, as she favored her second-born son. *Toldot* was a quagmire of complexity and paradox.

"Over the past few months, I've been learning about what it means to be part of a family," began Joseph, looking at his proud mom, teary-eyed dad, and smiling siblings, sitting in rapt attention in the front row of the synagogue. Next, he turned to the head of the congregation.

"Rabbi Weiss asked me to think about whether I identify more with Esau or Jacob. And the answer, I think, is both. We all have our good moments and bad ones. It's about how the choices we make define who we are and who we'll be.

"I think the 'two nations' in Rebekah's womb are like the two faces of America today—one that wants to build walls, and one that wants to reach out and help the underdog. That's what my father always does," said Joseph, staring at his dad, who was on the verge of losing it. "He helps those in need. It's a quality he inherited from his grandmother Sophie, who I've been reading about. Even though she came from impoverished roots in Russia, my great-grandmother would always lend a hand to others.

"Isn't that what the 'American Dream' is really about? It's not about making it and hoarding it. It's about reaching out to help the next person in line. The 'American Dream' is about giving rather than taking. It's about giving back.

"That's my takeaway from *Toldot*," concluded Joseph, folding up his notes and looking his father in the eye. Right on cue, John began to bawl. And (right on cue) Lani handed her husband the tissues she'd prepared for this exact moment.

Chapter 31

We the People

Tuesday, November 6, 2018, was a balmy day in Corpus Christi. The sun shone down from a cloudless sky with temperatures in the low eighties. And yet an insidious, invisible cloud seemed to be blanketing the city—so thick it could smother you. Not weather, but tension. It was Election Day.

Four days earlier, Federal Judge Nelva Gonzales Ramos had issued a ruling in Ralph Trent's motion, in which the incumbent congressman had petitioned the court to terminate Patti Alvarado's candidacy on the grounds that she was not a legal citizen. Ramos's decision was unsurprising: dismissal for lack of cause. But, also unsurprisingly, it had further divided the already highly polarized electorate.

Republicans cried foul. A Hispanic judge who labeled herself an unabashed Democrat; of course she'd sided with Alvarado. Even worse, Judge Ramos had been appointed by Obama—himself not native-born according to the "birthers," and therefore illegally elected in their view. It didn't help matters that Judge Ramos had ruled against a Texas voter ID law the prior year, declaring it unconstitutional on the grounds that it discriminated against minority voters. Her decision had been overturned, however, by the Fifth Circuit Court of Appeals in a 2–1 vote—two Republican appointees, against a dissenting Democrat.

Could our nation be more divided? John shook his head and sighed, gazing at the mob of seething protestors holding placards outside the polling station and shouting: "Lock her up! Lock her up!"

In the wake of Judge Ramos's ruling, Ralph Trent had taken to the airwaves in a media blitz to mobilize his base and get them out in numbers in pop-up protests at polling places, intended, of course, to intimidate and suppress the Hispanic turnout. Was it working?

John exchanged an anxious glance with Juliette, who'd accompanied him to Corpus Christi on this momentous day. They stepped out of the car, along with Patti and Enrique, here to cast their ballots. The protestors, upon seeing the object of their vitriol, went ballistic.

"Lock her up! Lock her up!"

"Go home to Mexico where you belong, bitch!"

"You can't steal our country!"

They were all male, all white—though their skin seemed to be turning beet red in anger.

Is that why they call them rednecks? wondered Juliette, worried that the situation was about to erupt into violence. She could see the veins bulging in those flushed necks.

"Back off!" shouted Enrique, escorting his wife to the polling place, where the media converged, almost more aggressively than the protestors. John could feel his adrenaline surging as reporters called out questions intended to provoke.

"How do you feel about reports that illegal aliens are pouring over the border to vote fraudulently and hijack the election?"

"Is your husband likely to relapse, given all this tension?"

Enrique looked like he was going to slug the guy but somehow kept his cool as he and Patti were given their ballots and entered adjacent booths. John took the opportunity to ask one of the news producers about exit polling thus far. It was close enough, apparently, for John to grab his daughter's hand in exuberance.

"What?" she asked.

"Nothing," he whispered. "Don't want to jinx it."

It was still morning, after all. Hours to go before they actually started counting votes. And later voting, particularly absentee ballots, tended to favor Republicans.

They went back to the Alvarado ranch and waited—watching news feeds, both local and national. John placed nonstop calls to people in the field. Turnout in the Latino precincts was at a record-breaking pace—lines out the door. Enrique paced like a caged lion. Juliette bit her nails. So did Patti—and hers were manicured. She did this while calling through a list of voters as part of her GOTV—get-out-the-vote—program.

When 8 p.m. rolled around and polls had closed, suddenly Patti started shutting off the TVs. "Enough!" she shouted. "We won't hear results for at least an hour. No more screens!" She crossed to Juliette and asked: "Have you ever made tamales?"

Patti got the household to agree to a media and device blackout until 9 p.m., when early absentee votes and precincts would be counted. She summoned everyone into the kitchen, where they created a tamale assembly line. Juliette joined Alexa at the stovetop to begin the filling—beans, veggies, and shredded chicken—while the men mixed up the masa dough. There were salsas to make, too—one green, one red.

"It's a family recipe," explained Patti. "Goes back generations."

Juliette nodded. "At our house, we still make Great-Grandma Rose's challah and brisket."

Generations, thought John. *Toldot*. It was hard to believe that less than one week earlier they'd been attending Joseph's bar mitzvah. He felt a tinge of sadness at how fleeting it was sometimes—these moments that seemed to take forever to arrive, then passed so quickly. Like elections.

Don't cling, he thought, remembering the lines of William Blake: "He who binds himself to a joy/Does the winged life destroy/He who kisses the joy as it flies/Lives in eternity's sunrise."

Part of John's melancholy stemmed from the fact that Joseph

Rakow's memoir was no more—they'd read the final chapter. It was just like *Toldot*, the story of Esau and Jacob, in that the narrative concluded upon the tacit reconciliation between the brothers—Max coming around to see Joseph's viewpoint and making a gesture toward his prolabor roots. But there was so much more to the story.

John observed Alexa showing Juliette how to shred the cooked chicken between two forks.

Watching his daughter work with her hands, he was reminded of his grandmother Rose and felt compelled to say: "You know, after Rose taught my mother the family brisket recipe, she'd often cook like this for the union meetings."

Juliette lit up. "Really? Great-Grandpa Joe continued his union organizing?"

"Till the day he died," said John. "It's all coming back to me."

He suddenly remembered a long-forgotten story that his mother Saralie used to tell them as kids of her earliest memory—being lifted up onto the podium at union meetings, where her father, Joseph, would be orating impassioned speeches to crowds of cheering workers.

Patti nodded. "That's what it's all about, isn't it? The legacy we leave for our children."

"Tamales!" grinned Alexa.

"And I thought you said you knew nothing of your family's history," remarked Patti.

John shrugged. "I'm learning."

"Nine o'clock!" Enrique shouted, then dived for the nearest TV.

Everyone held their breath. "My G-d," whispered Juliette. She was seeing it on her phone.

So was John. Their expressions were incredulous.

"It's the end of an era," said the TV news anchor in disbelief, and Alexa practically screamed. "By less than two thousand votes, newcomer Patti Alvarado has defeated incumbent Ralph Trent, becoming the first-ever formerly undocumented immigrant to win a seat in the Congress of the United States of America!"

They danced, they cheered, they hollered. Enrique was practically sobbing for joy as he hugged his wife.

He's like me, thought John, who was crying, too—in exaltation. And relief!

Juliette hugged her father with all her might. They stared at each other, letting it sink in.

Could the Alvarados actually be going to Washington? "He's going to demand a recount," John cautioned.

"Let him," smirked Patti. "We'll be making tamales."

Epilogue

And they did. But in Virginia, not Corpus Christi.

After the recount confirmed the election results, Patti Alvarado—with her fearless beginner's mind and tireless gumption—became one of the most charismatic "freshwomen" in Congress. Top of her agenda was reforming the Draconian laws that permit summary deportations without hearings, splitting families at the border, and the blanket banning of certain nationals from entrance into the United States. She promised Rose that she'd look into Bijan's case—and she did. They filed an appeal with the Department of Homeland Security to have the Yadzanis removed from their terrorist watch list. A judge would soon review the case, which would certainly be helped by having a sitting congresswoman as a character witness. With renewed hope, Rose and Bijan resumed their regular FaceTime calls—discussing everything from pimples to poetry.

John, for his part, had his own renewal, experiencing an incredible infusion of energy in his career as a Democratic campaign advisor. He'd achieved the unthinkable—unseating an eight-term incumbent in a largely conservative district with a scrappy, underfunded campaign.

John's stock soared. The phone started ringing. But John stopped answering it after 6 p.m. That was MFD—mandatory family dinner.

Acknowledgments

Everyone has a book inside of them. Personally, I just never thought that I'd ever write one. In college, it was all I could do to finish essays on time. Not that I didn't enjoy writing— I loved it. Unfortunately, I always preferred doing my own thing—penning a short story, a poem, or just an angry letter to the editor. I've had so little time in my professional life to even read books, let alone write any. But writing this book was something different. It was truly a labor of love. Love for my family—past and present. Love for those whose courage and persistence have inspired me to commit myself to Tikun Olam: To heal and change the world for the better.

First, I want to thank my dad and mom—Bill and Saralie Shallman. To my father, family always came first. He was orphaned at a young age, passed from relative to relative, from school to school—eventually joining the Marine Corp at the age of seventeen. A lifetime of service to his country, a PhD and marathon runner, Dad was always busy, but absolutely dedicated to ensuring his wife and five children had something he never had—the security of a stable, loving, and dependable home. Dad, you are a great father, and I'm so thankful to have you in my life and in the lives of my kids.

As I look back, I was blessed to have had the privilege of spending many hours last year with my mom before she died in February of 2020. I remember sitting at her kitchen table with a MacBook Pro as she regaled me with stories of her father while my fingers happily danced to the melody of her voice. I can never forget seeing her face change as Grandpa Joe's freshly translated words were finally revealed. After a lifetime of blissful ignorance to her father's tortured early years of life in Siberia, it was like seeing someone discover the wreckage of the Titanic. I could see her eyes travel back to a distant place and time—elated at hearing her father's words read for the first time in English by her son, wincing at the often bleak and brutal existence that eventually shaped the man who would become her kind, gentle, revolutionary father. Truth is, my mom is the true heroine of this epic adventure, her dad's heroic quest for the American Dream—one that has called so many in her family and now is calling her children's and grandchildren's names.

I love you, Mom. Thank you for all your love. Thank you for all your stories. Thank you for all the light and love and life you gave us. Through your children and grandchildren, you will live with us forever and ever.

I must, of course, thank the other important woman in my life: my amazing wife, Lani— a voracious reader and gentle critic who has stood by my side and encouraged me throughout this process, as she has for the past thirty years of marriage. I want to thank my four incredible blessings we call children, Ariana Rose, Nina Juliette, Benjamin Joseph, and Jonah Samuel. You are truly the lights in my life, and I love each of you with all of my heart and soul. I hope that I have helped guide you toward a future worthy of your dreams.

A special thank-you to my daughter Nina, the Amherst College–educated poet, singer, and songwriter who wrote a resplendent love poem for Joseph to Rosa. You truly captured your great-grandfather's romantic voice in a way only another dreamy romantic could.

To my sisters—Nancy and Debra—and to my brothers—Morty and

Danny—I love you guys. How special it is to be such good friends, who love one another unconditionally and generously. We truly are our mother's children.

A very special thanks to a few of my teachers and mentors along the way. To Mrs. Wisley and Mrs. Carlson, at Eugene Field Elementary School in Rock Island, Illinois. To Mr. Ostrom, Mr. Motz, Mr. Dennis, and Mr. Milton, at Rock Island High School. And, of course, thank you to Mrs. Shirley Rowland—an incredible drama teacher, director, and mentor. Thank you also to Rabbi and Professor Jay Holstein (the coolest Jew I've ever met), who taught a life-transforming course at the University of Iowa called Quest for Human Destiny that continues to inspire me as a reader, a writer, and a human being.

Thank you to the Yiddish Book Center for introducing me to the amazing Hershl Hartman—Yiddish translator extraordinaire. You saved me years of having to expand my Yiddish vocabulary beyond putz and shmuck and provided me with more than just my grandfather's words, but also his voice.

Thank you to the brilliant John Ridley, who inspired me to do more than just publish my grandfather's manuscript, but to seize this moment and write a book that explores my life in politics while also paying homage to his incredible story.

Thank you to the many teachers, rabbis, and cantors from the Tri-City Jewish Center in Rock Island. Thank you to Rabbi Feinstein and all of the magnificent rabbis of Valley Beth Shalom in Encino. I so would have wanted to share this with Rabbi Shulweis but am fortunate to have his esteemed colleagues in my corner and my family's corner always.

Thank you to all my friends and family, near and far. Every one of you helped to make me who I am today, and I hope this book makes you as proud of me as I am to have had you all in my life.

Last, but not least, thank you to the only grandparent I ever knew: Rose Rakow. My Grandma Rose taught me how to bake challah, play gin rummy, hem my own bell-bottom jeans, and, most important, to love with great passion and value family over anything. I love you, Grandma. Take good care of my mom.